FORTRESS • 90

GREEK FORTIFICATIONS OF ASIA MINOR 500–130 BC

From the Persian Wars to the Roman Conquest

KONSTANTIN S NOSSOV ILLUSTRATED BY BRIAN DELF

Series editors Marcus Cowper and Nikolai Bogdanovic

First published in 2009 by Osprey Publishing
Midland House, West Way, Botley, Oxford OX2 0PH, UK
443 Park Avenue South, New York, NY 10016, USA
E-mail: info@ospreypublishing.com

ISBN: 978 1 84603 415 2
E-book ISBN: 978 1 84908 128 3

Editorial by Ilios Publishing Ltd, Oxford, UK (www.iliospublishing.com)
Cartography: Map Studio, Romsey, UK
Page layout by Ken Vail Graphic Design, Cambridge, UK (kvgd.com)
Typeset in Myriad and Sabon
Index by Alison Worthington
Originated by PPS Grasmere, Leeds, UK
Printed in China through Bookbuilders

09 10 11 12 13   10 9 8 7 6 5 4 3 2 1

A CIP catalogue record for this book is available from the British Library.

ACKNOWLEDGEMENTS AND PICTURE CREDITS

The author wishes to express sincere thanks to Vladimir Golubev or preparing the line drawings that appear in this book.

All the photographic illustrations in this book are from the author's collection. All reproduction requests should be addressed to: konst-nosov@mtu-net.ru or konstantin_nossov@yahoo.com.

ARTIST'S NOTE

Readers may care to note that the original paintings from which the colour plates in this book were prepared are available for private sale. All reproduction copyright whatsoever is retained by the Publishers. All enquiries should be addressed to:

Brian Delf, 7 Burcot Park, Burcot, Abingdon, OX14 3DH, UK

The Publishers regret that they can enter into no correspondence upon this matter.

THE FORTRESS STUDY GROUP (FSG)

The object of the FSG is to advance the education of the public in the study of all aspects of fortifications and their armaments, especially works constructed to mount or resist artillery. The FSG holds an annual conference in September over a long weekend with visits and evening lectures, an annual tour abroad lasting about eight days, and an annual Members' Day.

The FSG journal *FORT* is published annually, and its newsletter *Casemate* is published three times a year. Membership is international. For further details, please contact:

The Secretary, c/o 6 Lanark Place, London W9 1BS, UK

Website: www.fsgfort.com

THE WOODLAND TRUST

Osprey Publishing are supporting the Woodland Trust, the UK's leading woodland conservation charity, by funding the dedication of trees.

FOR A CATALOGUE OF ALL BOOKS PUBLISHED BY OSPREY MILITARY AND AVIATION PLEASE CONTACT:

Osprey Direct, c/o Random House Distribution Center,
400 Hahn Road, Westminster, MD 21157
E-mail: uscustomerservice@ospreypublishing.com

Osprey Direct, The Book Service Ltd, Distribution Centre,
Colchester Road, Frating Green, Colchester, Essex, CO7 7DW
E-mail: customerservice@ospreypublishing.com

www.ospreypublishing.com

CONTENTS

GREEK FORTIFICATIONS OF ASIA MINOR 500–130 BC

INTRODUCTION

Greek tribes began moving into Asia Minor as early as the end of the 2nd millennium BC. The Aeolians were the first to arrive. They settled in the north-west part of Asia Minor creating the region of Aeolis bordering on Troad. The Aeolians were followed by the Ionians, who settled in the central part of the western coastal area of Asia Minor, giving this region its name, Ionia. The greatest Ionian city was Miletus and, in turn, its citizens founded a large number of colonies on the coasts of the Aegean and the Black Sea. The last to come were the Dorians, who, having occupied continental Greece, began colonizing the Greek islands and the coast of Asia Minor; they created the region of Doris (a small part of Caria). All these regions of Asia Minor populated by Greeks were close to continental Greece in cultural terms, save for the occasional peculiarity accounted for by the fact that they had powerful eastern states as their near neighbours. Many Greeks also populated the border regions of Caria, Mysia, Pamphylia, Troad and others, especially following the occupation of Asia Minor by Alexander the Great.

By the end of the first half of the 1st millennium BC there were numerous large Greek cities on the coast of western Anatolia; however, all of them, with the exception of Miletus, were annexed in the mid-6th century BC by the Lydian king Croesus. After the latter's death in 546 BC and following the Persian occupation of Lydia, the Ionian cities tried to regain their independence, but their uprising was quickly put down by the Persian army led by Harpagus. Nevertheless, the Ionians did not submit and often rose up in arms against the occupying forces. The greatest insurrection began in Miletus in 499 BC, leading to the intervention of Athens and Eritrea. The insurgents seized Sardis, the former capital of Lydia, but were soon defeated by the Persians on land and at sea (in the battle of Lade). In 494 BC Miletus fell and Ionia found itself under Persian rule again. Meanwhile, the Persian king decided to settle the score with Athens for its support of the insurrection, which led to the outbreak of the Persian Wars.

A new stage in the history of Greek colonies in Anatolia and Asia Minor began with the arrival of Alexander the Great. In spring 334 BC Alexander crossed the Dardanelles and in the course of six months swept along the whole of the western Anatolian coast, liberating one Greek city after another from their Persian garrisons. The sieges of Miletus and Halicarnassus turned out to be especially difficult for him. Asia Minor was brought into Alexander's empire, and after his death in 323 BC found itself first under the power of his general and successor Antigonus I, before passing to Lysimachus and later to Seleucus I. The huge Seleucid empire had already begun to disintegrate in the first half of the 3rd century BC. Western Anatolia saw the rise of the city of Pergamon, which became the capital of the independent Pergamonic kingdom (282–133 BC). This powerful kingdom played a significant role not only in Asia Minor but also in the whole of the Mediterranean. It was almost constantly at war with the Seleucid state, Macedonia, and the Galatians (Gauls). In the Second Macedonian War (200–197 BC) and a conflict between the Seleucidans and Rome (192–188 BC) the kings of Pergamon allied themselves with Rome, and in 188 BC were awarded a large part of western Asia Minor. According to the will of the last Pergamonic king Attalus III, the kingdom passed under the power of Rome in 133 BC, forming the province of Asia. During the First Mithridatic War almost all of Asia Minor found itself under the Kingdom of Pontus; later, however, the Romans regained control of it. Pergamon remained the capital of the province of Asia until 29 BC, when Ephesus replaced it.

By the time the Greeks had appeared in Asia Minor, fortification could already boast a long history in the Near East in general and Anatolia in particular. The Greek immigrants arrived too late to see the powerful Hittite empire in its prime, when it covered most of Asia Minor, and in particular the fortifications of Hattusha that stretched for many kilometres in the 13th century BC. They may, however, have come across the heirs of this great empire – the late Hittite kingdoms, that existed between 1180 and 700 BC – and, consequently, the fortifications of such cities as Karatepe or Sam'al (Zincirli). The 8th century BC saw Greek migrants occupy the site of deserted Troy. Founding a settlement known today as Troy VIII, they included the defensive walls of Troy VI/VII into the newly erected Greek works. Close contacts between Greeks and Egyptians began under Psamtik I (664–610 BC). Around 630–620 BC a Greek commercial base – Naukratis – appeared in the Nile delta. According to Strabo [17.801f], 30 ships came here from Miletus under the same Psamtik I to build a fortification at the mouth of the Nile. Of even more importance is the fact that Psamtik I hired Greek mercenaries. Carian and Ionian mercenaries played a significant role in the Egyptian army under the heirs of Psamtik I as well. A detachment of Greek mercenaries participated in the Egyptian march against the Kingdom of Kush (Nubia) in 593 or 591 BC. Mercenaries left evidence of their stay in Nubia, scratching graffiti on the legs of the colossi of Ramesses II that stand in front of the Temple of Abu Simbel. Before the Aswan dam was built, the monument stood in the area of the second cataract. So, it is almost certain that professional Greek warriors became acquainted with the formidable fortifications of Buhen and other Egyptian forts in the region. At least one precedent, in the use of Greek mercenaries by the Neo-Babylonian empire, is known. We should also keep in mind the military heritage of Ancient Greece – the Mycenaean citadels, long-deserted by the period under discussion here, were still admired by the Greeks for their powerful presence.

The fortifications of the Near East were built from two kinds of material: stone and mud-brick, sometimes exclusively using one of them, but more often using a combination of the two. In the latter case, a socle was made from stone and topped with a mud-brick superstructure that had a battlemented parapet. The mud-brick superstructure was strengthened by a timber-framed construction. The correlation of a stone socle and mud-brick work varied. A wall could be of mud-brick of half the height, or have only a mud-brick parapet. A combination of a stone socle and a mud-brick superstructure is characteristic

A tower on the eastern side of Perge. Most towers in this city have a blind ground floor, with slits appearing only from the second storey upwards. This tower, however, has slits at ground-floor level too, probably to provide better protection for the nearby postern.

of Hittite fortresses, Troy VI and Mycenaean citadels. In Mesopotamia and Egypt fortifications were chiefly built entirely of either mud-brick or stone. A distinctive feature of the Mycenaean citadels is the so-called 'cyclopean masonry', referring to the use of huge unworked or lightly worked stone boulders weighing several tons. Later Greeks believed that only the one-eyed Cyclops had strength enough to handle such immense boulders, hence the name. The stones were laid without mortar or clay; the space between the boulders was filled with small stones. The wall was of composite construction: the hollow spaces between the inner and outer layers of megalithic masonry were filled with rubble and earth. The thickness of such a stone wall reached 8m and more. The outer face of the stone wall in Troy VI was slightly inclined to the interior, as distinct from the strictly vertical walls of the Mycenaean fortresses. The walls of Troy VI were provided with vertical offsets varying in depth from 10 to 30cm and placed regularly at intervals of slightly over 9m. These offsets allowed the builders to slightly alter the direction of the walls without the use of corners, which presented a weak spot in the fortifications. Hittite fortifications were characterized by the casemate structure of a stone socle: the outer and inner walls were divided by crosswalls at regular intervals. The resultant rectangular cells were filled with earth or stones. The structure was not a Hittite innovation, as it is to be found in pre-Hittite Anatolia settlements, for instance, the 18th-century BC fortifications in Alishar. Numerous square towers are typical of Hittite and Mesopotamian fortresses. A parapet in Near-Eastern fortifications was usually crowned with semicircular or triangle-graded merlons.

Two towers in Heracleia on Latmus. The bottom storeys of the towers of the city defences were pierced by slits or windows, while the upper storeys featured large windows. The former seem to have housed arrow-firing devices, the latter stone-throwing ones.

The locations of the key sites featured in this book

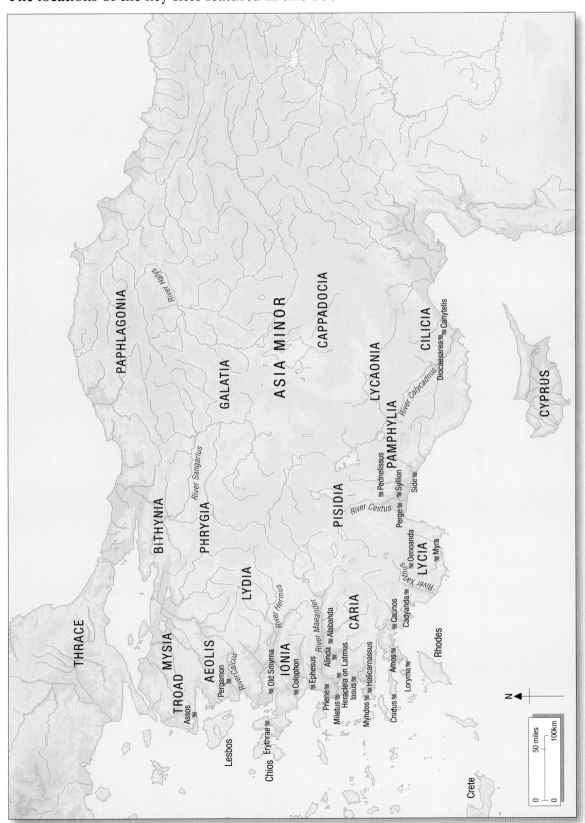

THRACE

PAPHLAGONIA

River Halys

GALATIA

ASIA MINOR

CAPPADOCIA

LYCAONIA

CILICIA

Diocaesarea

Canytelis

CYPRUS

River Calycadnus

BITHYNIA

River Sangarius

PHRYGIA

PISIDIA

Pednelissus

PAMPHYLIA

River Cestus

Perge

Syllion

Side

MYSIA

TROAD

AEOLIS

Pergamon

River Caicus

LYDIA

River Hermus

Old Smyrna

Colophon

IONIA

Ephesus

River Maeander

Priene

Alinda

Alabanda

Miletus

Heracleia on Latmus

Iasus

CARIA

Myndos

Halicarnassus

Caunos

Cadyanda

Oenoanda

LYCIA

River Xanthus

Myra

Assos

Lesbos

Chios

Erythrae

Cnidus

Amos

Loryma

Rhodes

Crete

N

0   50 miles

0   100km

How did the Near-Eastern fortifications and the Mycenaean citadels influence the Greek art of fortification? The destruction of the Mycenaean citadels in the early 12th century BC marked the arrival of a Dark Age for Greece. The art of fortification fell into decay. The Archaic period brought some improvements to the situation, but even now Greek fortifications continued to be primitive and lagged far behind the sophisitication of their Near-Eastern contemporaries. In defence, terrain was chiefly relied upon; fortifications ran along steep hill slopes, a rocky coastline, and so on. They usually comprised just a rampart built from roughly worked stones and topped with a mud-brick superstructure. At weak points the walls were strengthened with rare, single-storey towers or bastions or, occasionally, with jogs (projecting points); the Greeks still knew nothing of multi-storey towers proper or a specially made indented trace. The fortifications of Old Smyrna and Melia in Asia Minor offer an example of such simple defences. They date from just before 800 BC. Both settlements resemble the Mycenaean citadels in their principle of defence: walls of mud-brick on a stone socle curving convexly and following the terrain, and with a gate placed between dislocated walls or strengthened by a projecting spur (a single-storey tower or bastion). In the 6th century BC, probably under the influence of the East, stone walls began to be better laid and classically shaped rectangular towers (instead of occasional single-storey platforms as per the Mycenaean citadels) appear along their perimeter. During the 5th century BC the Greeks continued to experiment and absorb eastern influences, which affected Greek settlements in Asia Minor the most. Their efforts resulted in a distinctive Greek style of fortification that first appeared in the early 4th century BC.

CHRONOLOGY

499–494 BC	The Ionian Revolt takes place.
494 BC	Fall of Miletus. The last of the Greek cities on the western coast of Anatolia finds itself under Persian power.
499–479 BC	The Persian Wars – a series of wars between Greece and Persia.
395 BC	Tissaphenes, Persian satrap of Lydia and Caria, is killed. After his death a reorganization of the Anatolian provinces occurs. Some of them, Caria for instance, become relatively independent satrapies ruled by local, instead of Persian, potentates.
377–353 BC	Rule of Mausolus, satrap of Caria. He gains relative independence from Persia, and conquers a large part of Lycia, Ionia and several Greek islands. He makes Halicarnassus his capital and surrounds it with *c.* 7km-long walls.
334 BC	Alexander the Great crosses the Dardanelles and frees the Greek cities from their Persian garrisons.
323 BC	Death of Alexander the Great. Alexander's successors divide his empire into several parts.
323–281 BC	The Wars of Alexander's Successors.
312–64 BC	Seleucid dynasty, founded by Seleucus I, general and successor to Alexander the Great.

311 BC	Armistice in the Wars of Alexander's Successors. Asia Minor and Greece pass to Antigonus I, and Seleucus I receives a vast territory to the east of the Euphrates as far as India. In the same year Ptolemy takes Cilicia from Antigonus I and war breaks out again.
305–304 BC	The famous siege of Rhodes, which is allied to Ptolemy, by Demetrius Poliorcetes (Antigonus' son). Demetrius uses a large number of siege machines, of impressive variety and size, but fails to seize the city.
301 BC	The battle of Ipsus. The coalition of the successors defeats the army of Antigonus I. The latter is killed in battle. The victors divide Antigonus' possessions. Most of Asia Minor goes to Lysimachus.
297 BC	The ruler of Bithynia (in the north-west of Asia Minor) defeats Alexander's successors Lysimachus and Seleucus I and declares it an independent state.
296 BC	Lysimachus takes Caria from Demetrius Poliorcetes and joins it to his possessions in Asia Minor.
282 BC	The commandant of Lysimachus in Pergamon hands the city over to Seleucus I.
282–133 BC	The Pergamonic kingdom.
281 BC	Seleucus I defeats Lysimachus in the battle at Corupedium. Lysimachus is killed and his possessions in Asia Minor pass to Seleucus I. On his way to Macedonia Seleucus I is killed.
278 BC	Nicomedes I, King of Bithynia, employs a Gaulish army (the Galatians) to fight his insurgent brother. After the war the Galatians disperse through Asia Minor, devastating the countryside for some 50 years until they are defeated by a Pergamonic king. They are forced to settle in the area that is named after them – Galatia.
264 BC	Nicomedes builds Nicomedia, the capital of Bithynia.
200–197 BC	The Second Macedonian War.
188 BC	A large part of western Asia Minor is annexed by the Pergamonic kingdom.
183 BC	The Pergamonic kingdom annexes Galatia.
168–167 BC	A great uprising of the Galatians threatens the Pergamonic kingdom.

Two towers in the west wall of the lower town at Perge. The acropolis, sitting on a high plateau, can be seen in the background. No fortifications of the acropolis survive; however, a row of towers and considerable sections of the curtains have been preserved in the lower town.

Founded in the 7th century BC, Side was a prospering city in the Hellenistic period. It owed its prosperity to its advantageous position, which prompted Cilician pirates to turn it into their naval base and slave-trade centre. The city was encircled by defensive walls some time between 225 and 188 BC. Only fragments of the land wall protecting the peninsula on the side of the mainland survive. The reconstruction of the shoreline walls is hypothetical. The later structures of the Roman and Byzantine periods, which can be viewed at the site today but were not there in the 2nd century BC, are not shown in this reconstruction.

166 BC	The Roman Senate declares Galatia an independent country.
133 BC	In line with the will of the last Pergamonic king Attalus III, the territory of the Pergamonic kingdom passes under the power of Rome. This is the official date of the formation of the Roman province of Asia. However, the real power of Rome over western Anatolia is only firmly established in 130 BC, after Aristonicus' rising is put down.
133–129 BC	An insurrection of slaves and the poor in Pergamon, headed by Aristonicus. In 131 BC Aristonicus defeats the Roman legions facing him, but in 130 BC he is beaten by the Romans. In 129 BC he is taken prisoner, brought to Rome and executed.
88–85 BC	The First Mithridatic War. Mithridates VI Eupator drives the Romans out of Asia Minor and invades Greece. By the end of the war the Roman army, led by Sulla, forces Mithridates to enter negotiations and return the Roman possessions in Asia Minor.
83–81 BC	The Second Mithridatic War.
74 BC	Bithynia becomes a Roman province.
74–63 BC	The Third Mithridatic War.
67 BC	Pompey starts a large-scale operation against pirates, freeing the whole of the Mediterranean from them. The pirates' coastal bases in Asia Minor are destroyed. To defend the area from pirates forts are built, many of which are later turned into medieval castles.
64 BC	Bithynia and Pont are amalgamated into one province.
30 BC	Ptolemy's Egypt is included into the Roman state. This is the official date of the end of the Hellenistic period.
25 BC	Galatia is turned into a Roman province, with the capital in Ankira (modern Ankara).

THE PRINCIPLES OF DEFENCE

Types of fortification

Acropolis. As a rule, the acropolis (or citadel) lay atop a rock that towered over the city and was difficult to access. In Greece settlements of the Geometric period often had only a fortified acropolis; the lower city had no walls. In times of danger the inhabitants left their houses and sought shelter in the acropolis. By the classical and Hellenistic periods the city already had both an acropolis and city walls.

City walls. The earliest Greeks settlements on the coasts of Asia Minor and offshore islands had a fairly large fortified area but no citadel (acropolis). All the population lived in walled territories, so these settlements may be considered as fortified villages or towns. Later an acropolis was added to the city walls. The right of a city to defend itself by building fortifications was an important aspect of its independence. Alexander's proclamation of the independence of the Greek cities instigated the construction of urban fortifications on a great scale in Asia Minor in the late 4th century BC.

Fort (phrourion) and signal-tower. Garrisoned all year round, these small outposts served to inform the nearest city and the metropolis of the danger of invasion and to keep trade routes safe. They could also offer shelter to any endangered populations of neighbouring villages. Forts and outposts began to grow in number in the 5th century BC. In Asia Minor, many Greek forts and signal-towers were discovered in Caria, a region heavily fortified even by ancient standards. In Lycia, Myra East Fort or Isium is the best-known example. Greek mercenaries may have borrowed the idea of building forts in strategically important places from the Persians. Some 139 Persian forts dating mainly from the late 6th–mid-5th century BC have been discovered. Their number was obviously much greater. Placed along essential routes, an intricate network of them covered the entire Persian empire.

Private residential tower (tyrsis). In Asia Minor single towers of this type can be seen in Canytelis, Diocaesarea and Myra (at the Myra West Fort).

Fortified camp. The mainland wall in Iasus is a good example of this type of fortification.

Long walls. These protected a whole district, or connected a city and a harbour together. The best-known examples are in Greece, namely the Dema Wall and the walls connecting Athens and its port of Peiraieus.

Some types of fortification cannot be easily distinguished. Thus, some scholars consider the tower known as 'Myra West Fort' to be a private structure, others think it is a signal-tower. A single tower or even a fort could be built by a rich resident for his family or by local farmers and peasants to serve as public defence building. Whether a tower or a fort housed a garrison or a rich family or refugees, and whether its building was paid for with state or private or public means, is not always easy to determine. Some details are, however, significant. For instance, a tower standing in an area with poor lines of sight could hardly have served as a signalling station, while an olive press in the neighbourhood speaks in favour of its having been used by civilians.

TOP LEFT
This tower at Diocaesarea supposedly dates from the 3rd century BC. It is an excellent example of a *tyrsis*, a private residential tower. It originally had six storeys, but the upper storey has been destroyed. Each storey is partitioned into rooms.

TOP RIGHT
This detached, solitary tower in Canytelis/Kanytelleis is, like the tower at Diocaesarea, an example of a *tyrsis*, a private residential tower. The two towers are to be found in Cilicia, not far from each other. Both were erected not long before 200 BC, when the region was unsafe.

Methods of construction

The period in question is characterized by Greek fortifications built either from sun-dried mud-brick on a stone socle, or entirely from stone. Walls made entirely of mud-brick, which were common in ancient Mesopotamia and Egypt, were unpopular in Greece and Asia Minor, probably because of the increased rain or snow there, which could easily undermine them. Walls were safer in areas of wet soil when built on a stone socle. Compared to stone, mud-brick could be made using considerably less, and also unskilled, labour. Moreover, mud-brick structures were less susceptible to damage by earthquakes and by the blows inflicted during sieges. Nevertheless, the durability offered by all-stone walls made Greeks renounce mud-brick almost entirely. After 400 BC, only a few Greek cities in Asia Minor used mud-brick for building parapets (as at Pednelissus, Sillyon and Teos). All-stone fortifications clearly prevailed.

In his work *Greek Walls*, R. L. Scranton identified several styles of Greek masonry and grouped them in the chronological order in which they were used. His framework is still widely adhered to, although it has been slightly adapted by some scholars. The main points of Scranton's typology are as follows. Stonemasons could use unfinished rubble or carefully hewn blocks in construction. The latter is of more interest to us, as this type of masonry was used in Greek fortification of the period in question, and because it allows us to single out definitive styles. Carefully hewn masonry could be coursed or uncoursed. Coursed masonry included trapezoidal and ashlar-style stones, while uncoursed masonry included polygonal, curvilinear ('Lesbian masonry'), trapezoidal and ashlar styles. In coursed masonry the courses could either be of equal height (isodomic) or of differing height (pseudo-isodomic). In addition, in coursed masonry the blocks could all be laid as stretchers, or headers could be introduced at intervals ('header-and-stretcher courses'), or courses of headers could be alternated with courses of stretchers ('alternate header/stretcher courses').

R. L. Scranton's terminology is not ideal: trapezoidal and ashlar blocks are, strictly speaking, also polygonal. Moreover, one style is not always easily distinguished from another. Lesbian masonry differs from polygonal by having more rounded sides and better worked blocks. Trapezoidal blocks have parallel top and bottom sides, but their lateral sides are sloping.

Despite these small deficiencies, R. L. Scranton's typology sheds light on the evolution of building methods and the areas of popularity of the styles of masonry. Polygonal masonry, which was originally found mainly in the Peloponnese and western Greece, became widespread in mainland

Styles of masonry used in Greek fortification.
1: rubble.
2: uncoursed polygonal.
3: uncoursed Lesbian.
4: uncoursed trapezoidal.
5: uncoursed ashlar.
6: isodomic coursed trapezoidal, all stretchers.
7: isodomic coursed ashlar, header-and-stretcher courses.
8: pseudo-isodomic coursed ashlar, alternate header/stretcher courses.

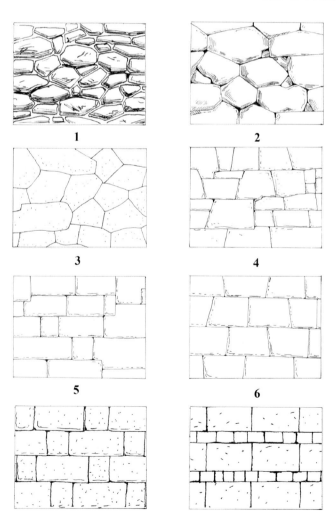

1

2

3

4

5

6

7

8

Greece between 480 and 400 BC. From the late 5th century BC it declined in popularity. The second half of the 4th century BC is marked in the Peloponnese by the appearance of a stylistic variant known as 'coursed polygonal', which differs from uncoursed polygonal only in the tendency to lay blocks in horizontal rows. Lesbian masonry was used in the Archaic period and in northern and eastern Greece, on the islands, and in Asia Minor. Uncoursed trapezoidal masonry became widespread after the Persian Wars. It was later replaced by coursed trapezoidal masonry, which remained fashionable throughout the late 5th and the 4th centuries BC. The end of the 5th century saw experiments with uncoursed ashlar; this gave birth to coursed ashlar masonry, which became the dominant style from the mid-4th century BC. Ashlar and trapezoidal pseudo-isodomic and header-and-stretcher systems are particularly characteristic of the Hellenistic period.

Scranton's conclusions on the whole hold true for Greece, the islands and Asia Minor, but some styles date from earlier. Thus, ashlar masonry, used in temple architecture from quite early times, was discovered in the fortifications of Old Smyrna (c.850–25 BC) and in Sardis, capital of the Lydian empire and later a most important city in the west of the Persian empire. This shows its popularity in the region before the 5th century BC. R. L. Scranton's chronology is problematic when considering Sicily and southern Italy. In the fortifications of the western Greek cities, Lesbian masonry does not seem to

ABOVE LEFT
Isodomic ashlar – rectangular blocks of stone laid in rows of the same height, in alternating header/stretcher courses. The rows alternate, first consisting of only headers, then of only stretchers. This example is from the round tower by the main gate in Perge.

ABOVE RIGHT
The city walls of Caunos. The space between the smooth outer and inner masonry faces is filled with rubble. The ancient harbour can be seen in the background.

The upper part of the U-shaped artillery tower at Assos. There is no infill between the masonry faces; either the upper part of the tower must have been considered solid and stable enough as it was, or the mud-brick once filling the space has by now disappeared. Walls of a similar structure can also be seen in Sillyon and Isaura.

be present; nor was the polygonal style popular, although it survived longer than in the Aegean world, while ashlar, used from the 7th century BC, was popular from the early 5th century BC onwards.

Within the defences of a single city, the walls could be laid in different styles. This can be explained by different periods of construction; repair works, for example, of a section damaged in a siege; different groups of masons each using their favourite styles; aesthetic considerations, such as a desire to archaize walls (a particularly typical tendency in Asia Minor, where polygonal masonry can be found throughout the Hellenistic period and even up to the late 1st century AD in Roman Lycia); and, finally, different designations of defensive structures. In Halicarnassus, for instance, the masonry of the curtains differs from that of the towers, despite the fact that they were built at the same time. One possible explanation for this is the greater significance attached to towers. Lacking the capacity to enfilade the attacking enemy, the latter often became the chief target for assault and had to withstand battering, mining and so on. From the 4th century BC onwards, towers had to become stronger in order to accommodate artillery.

Polygonal and Lesbian masonry, though very handsome and providing better cohesion, were the most time-consuming to erect, as the sides of the blocks had to be neatly adjusted. Therefore, they were used in small fortresses as architectural 'showpieces', such as gateways, or for rebuilding certain sections. These styles continued to be used in these ways down into Hellenistic times. However, where fortifications of considerable length needed to be built in a short time, regular isodomic masonry, be it trapezoidal or ashlar, was preferred.

Curtains were rarely laid using stone blocks throughout their entire depth, although such solid walls could be found. More commonly, the interior and exterior faces were made from carefully hewn stones, with the space between them filled with any cheap material that was to hand – rubble, gravel, and broken bricks mixed with earth or clay. Increased strength was achieved by filling the space between with materials of different sizes, for example rubble and earth, as it created an even infill of the space without much shrinkage. Mud-brick may have been occasionally used as a filling. It had doubtless advantages (it absorbed shock and exerted no outward pressure) but made the construction of a wall much more labour-consuming. Besides, mud-brick could be washed out with time. So-called 'hollow' walls (lacking any filling between the masonry faces) may have had mud-brick filling that disappeared later. On the other hand, these 'hollow' walls are only to be encountered in the walls of some towers, relatively thin curtains built on the edge of a high cliff, or in other places with difficult access, which may mean that the builders saw no need to provide any filling.

Walls laid using trapezoidal or ashlar masonry were made stronger by the presence of headers stretching into the fill. For better cohesion with the filling, the inner faces of the blocks were left rough and unworked. To increase safety, bonding courses were occasionally made at intervals. These bonding courses stretched through the whole thickness of the wall and usually projected slightly on either side, as for instance at Alinda and Alabanda.

The Greeks knew of mortar and used it in making cisterns and foundations. Philon [*Pol.*, I.1, I.8, I.11, I.20] recommended using mortar and iron clamps to build foundations and to fasten header blocks in place. In practice, however, mortar was not used in defensive structures (with the exception of the Hellenistic foundations at Dura Europos in Syria). The Greeks laid the facing blocks of defensive walls dry or with a thin layer of clay, imperceptible from the outside. Clay was also used as a binding material for infilling walls and for cementing rubble in fortifications of the Archaic period (for example, at Old Smyrna). Besieging Tyre in 332 BC the Greeks became acquainted with mortared stone walls, which looked higher and stronger to them than their own walls. No borrowing of building techniques followed, though. The Greeks probably discovered that mortared stone walls tended to fall down in huge masses under the impact of rams, mines, or earthquakes whereas Greek dry walls fell only at the point of stress, suffering merely localized damage.

DESIGN AND DEVELOPMENT

Around the middle of the 3rd century BC, possibly in the 240s, Philon wrote his work called the *Poliorketika*. It is the only surviving Hellenistic manual on fortification, and includes detailed recommendations on the ways city walls should be built and defended, as well as on the methods of attacking them. Philon was a military engineer; it is possible that he served in the Ptolemaic army and wrote this treatise for one of the commanders. In any case, it was not via hearsay that Philon learned about the art of fortification, and his field of knowledge as an engineer embraced missile-throwing machines as well, which is reflected in another treatise of his, the *Belopoeica*. Here we shall take a look at Philon's recommendations and consider to what extent and in which ways they were put into practice in Asia Minor. Unless otherwise indicated, all textual references in the following sections refer to his *Poliorketika*.

Curtains

Philon singles out three forms of curtain. Firstly, there are slanting curtains. In this system of fortification, which Philon considers the most useful [I.55–58], curtains adjoin towers either at an acute or at an obtuse angle. Philon recommends strengthening not only fortresses but also military camps in this way. A good example of this system of fortification can be found in the south cross-wall at Miletus.

Secondly, there is the 'saw-teeth trace' or indented trace, which, in Philon's opinion [I.44], should be supplemented by pentagonal towers. An example of this layout can be seen in the mainland wall at Iasus, where there are 32 jogs with 18 surviving towers. However, the towers in Iasus are semicircular, not pentagonal. The indented trace was usually built as a cheaper alternative to building towers, which could be dispensed with. The acute angle projecting towards the enemy allowed a jog in the wall to enfilade the adjoining curtains in two directions. An alternative system (*en crémaillère*), with jogs looking only onto one side, allowed the enfilading of just one adjoining curtain. However, the latter system proved equally justified when used on the slope of a hill, where the direction of enemy attack was fairly predictable. In Colophon, for instance, jogs probably protected the gate which stood lower down. Moreover, in such places the indented trace could provide for more effective tier-fire as compared with the more usual system of towers connected with each other by straight curtains. The curtain adjoining the outermost jog was usually protected by the tower standing at the very top of the hill. The indented trace was used at Alinda, Alabanda, Ephesus and Priene as well as in other locations too.

Thirdly, there are 'semicircular' (although in reality, they were sometimes merely concave) curtains connected by towers, which are placed so that the concave side faces the enemy [Philon, I.39–40]. The advantages of this

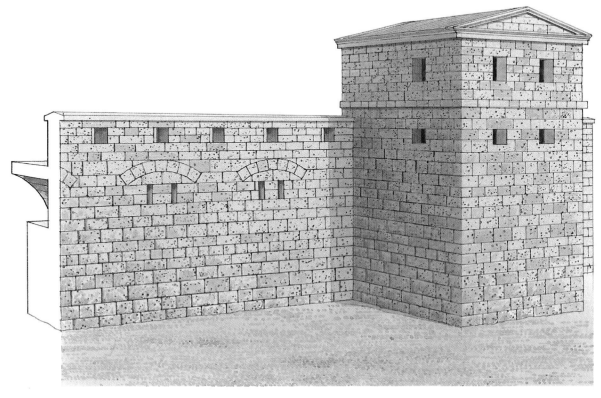

form of construction are obvious: with the towers projecting considerably outwards, the enemy troops attacking a curtain found themselves exposed to massive fire to the sides and the rear from both the towers and the angles of the curtains. This form of layout can be seen in the south wall of Dura Europos in Syria (3rd or 2nd century BC, with later changes). In Asia Minor a structure not unlike this one can be found at Side, where the curtains stand far behind the projecting towers and are connected with the latter by subsidiary walls. In 334 BC during the siege of Halicarnassus, the defenders erected a similar crescent-shaped, mud-brick wall beyond a breach.

Philon does not mention straight curtains between towers, though possibly implies their existence in the 'maeander trace' system. He must have considered they were something to be taken for granted, and that, in his manual, he only wished to present the latest and most interesting achievements in the art of fortification.

Structurally, curtains could be of one of four types:

1. Simple, single storey, crowned with a wall-walk on top. This was the oldest and most common type.

2. Single storey, but containing arched emplacements for missile-throwing engines (as at Miletus).

3. Two storey, with high arches and a lower wall-walk beyond the arches (as at Perge).

4. Three storey (with three tiers of fire), with arches below (as at Side).

The city wall of Priene, showing a jog in the wall. The jog allowed flanking fire to be brought to bear upon the space alongside the adjusting curtain, but, unlike with a tower, this was on one side only. A jog was a cheap alternative to a tower.
In Priene the south city wall was protected mostly by jogs, while along the rest of the walls there are towers.

B THE CURTAINS OF PERGE

Built in the late 3rd century BC, the fortifications of Perge were revolutionary for their time. The curtains are of two structural types: a simple solid wall, and a wall with buttresses, arches, a mural gallery and embrasures for arrow-firing devices. This illustration shows the latter type, from the interior and exterior. The wall provides two levels for the defence: an upper wall-walk, and a mural gallery. The former was wide enough to accommodate a three-span catapult, but the mural gallery was considerably narrower; there was only room for archers. It is possible, however, that temporary wooden planking was placed between the arches during a siege, allowing additional arrow-firing devices to be mounted here.

Philon [I.17–19] says that the fortress of Rhodes had curtains with arches, a wall-walk on the top and barracks for the garrison below. This has not yet been confirmed by excavation, but the general description resembles the curtains at Side or Perge.

Philon [I.11–12] recommends making curtains no thinner than 10 cubits (4.6m) and at least as high as 20 cubits (9.2m), so that any ladders placed against the wall could not reach its top. Indeed, ladders longer than 10m were considered too unwieldy and insecure, and the escalade of a fortress wall over 10m high with such ladders was believed to be impractical. In reality, curtains did not always reach 10m in height, and were often between 7m and 9m. The thickness of curtains was, in most cases, also less than that recommended by Philon, but thicker examples could occasionally be found.

A curtain was topped with a wall-walk. More often than not it was a permanent feature; only in exceptional cases, as for instance in Cadyanda, was a temporary wall-walk made of planks on buttresses beyond the curtain built, as recommended by Philon [I.15–16]. If a curtain was taken, the temporary planking could be removed and the enemy would be denied access into the city. Stone eaves were sometimes built in the upper rear part of a curtain in order to widen the wall-walk (as at Oenoanda, Pednelissus, Perge, Side, and Sillyon).

The parapet of a curtain could be crenellated (*epalxion*) or continuous with windows (*epalxis*). The proposition of F. Krischen [p. 51] that a parapet with merlons made way for *epalxis* in the late 4th century BC does not always hold true, as there are examples of later crenellated walls. Philon [I.14] insists that curtains should have battlements and a roof. The latter would be particularly important for curtains intended to accommodate artillery, such as those at Perge and Side.

In order to facilitate the repair of any sections damaged by stone-throwing engines, Philon [I.13] recommends that oak beams be included in curtains and towers every 1.8m. He also advises [I.10] that 60 cubits (27.7m) of space should remain clear of houses behind any fortifications in order to facilitate the transfer of troops and the delivery of stones, and to allow the digging of a ditch if need be. No such considerable space has yet been discovered anywhere; a vacant zone of 13.8m was identified at Rhodes and of 12.3m at Ephesus.

Towers

Philon mentions rectangular, semicircular, pentagonal and hexagonal towers. He recommends [I.3–4] placing rectangular, pentagonal and hexagonal towers so that they have one angle projecting to the outside. He believes not only that this disposition makes for better enfilade, but that it also diminishes the damage inflicted by enemy battering rams or stone-throwing engines. Philon [I.6] advises that gateways should be protected with hexagonal towers, being more solid than rectangular ones, and enabling missile-throwing engines to bring fire to bear in any direction.

In practice, rectangular towers were the most favoured in Greek fortification, although circular, semicircular, pentagonal, hexagonal and heptagonal-shaped ones can be found in their fortifications. Rectangular towers continued to dominate, though – possibly because they were cheaper and easier to construct. In Asia Minor circular and pentagonal towers appeared around the middle of the 4th century BC (Alabanda), semicircular ones towards the end of that century (Colophon, Heracleia), and hexagonal (Miletus), hepta- and octagonal (Isaura)

ones only as late as the Roman period in the 1st century BC. For all that, if circular and semicircular towers were relatively common, and semicircular ones were in some places even more numerous than rectangular ones (such as at Colophon and Iasus), pentagonal and other polygonal towers were always rare.

Semicircular towers were the second most popular type after rectangular ones. Philon [I.64–66] considered half-round towers to be exceptionally strong; built according to wooden models made prior to construction, they were capable of withstanding bombardment easily. He asserts that stones launched from missile-throwing machines would 'glance off [the towers] and the blocks would not give way at all, since they are wider on the outside than inwards'. It could also be added that semicircular (as well as circular and hexagonal) towers had wider fields of fire as compared with rectangular and pentagonal towers.

Most towers were filled with earth and rubble as high as the wall-walk level, improving their ability to withstand siege weapons. Only by undermining could such towers be brought down. If the upper storeys were destroyed, the raised platform remained in place to hamper access to the assailants. A storey provided with slits was created at the wall-walk level, with another one above it (in the artillery towers) that featured windows. A tower was topped with a roof or a fighting platform with a battlemented parapet. (Artillery towers were often covered with a roof to protect the engines from the uncertainties of weather; this, however, cannot be considered a general rule – there are artillery towers that feature a fighting platform on top.) Numerous exceptions from this kind of tower structure are known, though. For instance, towers with more storeys can be found. The middle storey could have windows as well as

ABOVE LEFT
The entrance to the U-shaped tower at Assos. This arched entrance is atypically large. It was probably especially designed to facilitate the accommodation of a catapult in the tower.

ABOVE RIGHT
A slit in the side of the U-shaped tower at Assos. The apertures seem wide when viewed from the outside, but they are hourglass-shaped in plan and are no more than 0.20m wide inside the wall. Hence, they could be used for firing arrows, but not for a stone-throwing device.

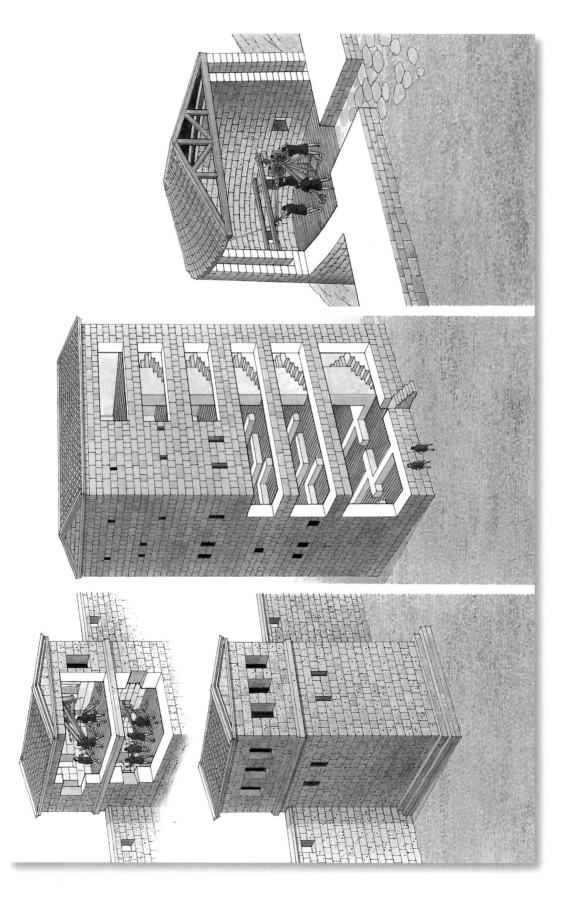

A tower in Heracleia on Latmus, viewed from the inside. The central windows on the lower storey were designed for small engines; there are slits for archers on the sides. The upper storey is provided with large windows for large missile machines.

slits, as, for example, at Heracleia on Latmus. The ground floor was often hollow, sometimes with slits (in Ephesus even with windows for engines), and sometimes blind. Apertures on the ground floor were made to increase firepower in particularly important sectors, especially if the bottom part of the tower was sufficiently protected by the terrain. Rooms without apertures were used for storage and as barracks for the guards.

A wall-walk ran either behind the towers or through them. A. W. McNicoll [1997, p. 13] believes that the former was common for artillery towers, while towers pierced with a wall-walk were not intended for artillery.

Doorways in artillery towers should be, according to Philon [I.25], as large as possible and arched, to facilitate the entry and exit of stone-throwing engines. A large arched doorway in a half-round tower in Assos fully conforms to his recommendation. Some artillery towers may have been open-backed or, at least, provided with large openings in their rear walls. This not only facilitated the movement of engines, but also allowed these towers to accommodate more powerful engines with their rear parts sticking out of the tower, sitting on the wall-walk or wooden scaffolding. Such towers are supposed to have existed at Heracleia on Latmus, Perge and Side, although this has not yet been confirmed.

Philon [I.20] recommends apertures that either widen towards the interior or that are narrow in the middle and shaved off in the lower portion. The latter, he says, are effective in making enemy missiles glance off. Three types of aperture

C TOWERS

(1) Perge, late 3rd century BC. This is a typical rectangular three-storey tower. The first storey is blind, the second is pierced by slits, and the upper storey has large windows (three in each projecting side). The tower could accommodate at least one five-mina stone-projector or several arrow-firing devices (1A). (2) The tower at Diocaesarea, 3rd century BC, an example of a *tyrsis* or private residential tower. Of its six storeys, three lower ones have five rooms each, and each of the three upper ones is partitioned into four rooms. Communication between the storeys was by a stone staircase. Two entrances led into the tower: one on the ground floor (in the southern wall), and the other on the second floor (in the eastern wall). (3) The U-shaped tower at Assos, late 3rd century BC. Built in the age of artillery, the tower radically differs from the other towers at Assos. It had a single chamber on a single floor, reached via an arched entrance. With the help of a system of pulleys, a catapult could be shifted to fire from any of the five embrasures in the tower.

An aperture for a small missile-throwing engine, probably an arrow-firing device at Heracleia on Latmus. The two apertures below, on either side of the window, are interesting. Only a few examples of such apertures are known in Greek fortification. Their purpose is unclear. One theory is that they were for the rods that pinned the shutters firmly to the wall. Perhaps a bottom-hinged, not a top-hinged, shutter was used here.

were possible: openings of equal thickness on the outside and inside (usually windows for artillery – only early engine windows were bevelled on one side, like the ones at Ephesus); openings that were wider on the inside than on the outside (characteristic of slits); and hourglass-shaped openings (that is, most narrow in the thickness of the wall but widening at both the front and rear faces). Hourglass-shaped slits can be seen in the artillery tower at Assos and in the private residential tower at Diocaesarea. The width of the windows in fortifications varied between 60cm and 90cm. Slits were usually 10–15cm wide on the outside and 50–60cm on the inside. Slits with a wider outside opening (for example, the *c*. 30cm-wide slits at Messene) were, in E. W. Marsden's opinion [pp. 128–30], earlier experimental apertures for arrow-firing devices; later slits were mainly used by archers, while windows were built for arrow-firing and stone-throwing devices. Windows were undoubtedly more convenient than slits for arrow-firing devices, and stone-throwing devices could only be fired through windows. Slits, however, continued to be used by arrow-firing devices later on, and windows began to appear at the same time as the first generation of artillery towers, as early as the first half of the 4th century BC. For instance, an artillery tower at Assos dating from the late 3rd century BC features a storey that is undoubtedly designed for artillery, with the maximum width of the slits in the thickness of the wall reaching 20cm. Therefore, storeys with slits could be used not only by archers, but to accommodate arrow-firing devices as well. Windows were sealed with shutters, thus protecting missile-throwing machines from bad weather during peacetime and artillerymen from enemy missiles during times of war.

According to Philon's instructions [I.62–63], towers should be independent structures, as a rule, only lightly bonded to the curtain. This can be explained, first, by the desire to localize any damage should the tower or the adjoining curtains collapse. Besides, towers were often added later, some time after the construction of the circuit walls. Inscriptions provide evidence to show that towers were occasionally paid for by donations from individuals or groups of people in order to modernize existing defences.

Gates and posterns

Philon does not give any special attention to gates. The most common type of gate in the Hellenistic period was a straight gateway flanked by two towers. Beyond the gate, most notably at Pamphylia, there was a fortified courtyard where enemy soldiers could be easily overcome if they broke through the gate.

Gate-towers like those at Pednelissus and Sillyon could occasionally be encountered, but they were built after 133 BC.

The presence of posterns or small gateways points to active defence. The more posterns, the more active the measures the defenders planned to undertake in case of a siege. The main purpose of posterns was naturally to allow the defenders to make sallies; facilitating communication between the city and the country during peacetime was only a minor consideration.

Posterns were easier to protect than gates, but for better protection they were usually placed in a tower or a jog or next to them. In the mainland wall of Iasus posterns were made in the lateral sides of all towers and in jogs. This system allowed soldiers in making a sally to act in full correspondence with Philon's recommendation [I.33]: they went out through a sally-port having their shielded side outwards and came back through another sally-port (in the next tower) without exposing the unshielded side. The return through another postern had an additional advantage: any departing and newly arriving sortie parties did not collide with each other. Philon advises [I.35] putting outer fortifications in front of a postern in order to protect it from stone-throwing engines and make it easier for the defenders to sally forth unnoticed. However, no such outer fortification dating precisely from Philon's time or earlier has yet been discovered.

As far back as the mid-4th century BC Aineias Tacticus [39.3–4] recommended making portcullises in the gates. So far, the earliest portcullises have been discovered in the sally-ports of the west wall at Dura Europos. F. E. Winter [pp. 265–67] suggests that a device resembling a portcullis was used in the outer gate of the gate-tower at Sillyon. It is true that, unlike movable grating, this device was not raised vertically but at an angle and, when raised, was located under the ceiling (the leaf of the gate rotated around a fixed upper beam). It is difficult to judge the usefulness of this structure. It could probably inflict casualties on the enemy if dropped. The inner gate in this tower was evidently closed with ordinary leaves hanging on the sides.

A gate-tower at Sillyon, viewed from inside the fortress. The gate is covered by a lintel (a row of trapezoidal blocks, to be exact) on the outside and by a true arch on the inside. The small windows on the first and second floors are unsuitable for large stone-throwing devices, so the defenders of the tower probably used arrow-firing ones.

A TOUR OF THE SITES

Three sites, Perge, Side and Sillyon, are examined in this chapter, their fortifications being the best preserved and most interesting from a structural point of view. All the sites exemplify city defences, but the fortifications differ in the time of their construction and the structures themselves. The sites are arranged according to the chronological sequence of construction.

Perge

Perge was the capital of the region of Pamphylia. This large city consisted of two fortified sites: the lower town, and the acropolis towering above it on a plateau. None of the fortifications of the acropolis survive. In contrast, the fortifications of the lower town, dating from the late 3rd century (possibly *c.* 225 BC), are very well preserved in places and are particularly interesting.

The curtains of Perge represent two types of structure. The first type, which can be seen in some sections of the western wall, is a simple wall 1.40–2m thick. This was crowned with a wall-walk occasionally placed on two or three courses of eaves. Rows of eaves allowed the wall-walk to be made wider, easier to move along, and thus more convenient for the defence, precluding the labour-hungry option of having to broaden the entire wall. The second type is a *c.* 2m-thick wall backed by *c.* 1.2m-thick buttresses. Placed about 4m apart from each other, the buttresses are crowned with arches topped with a wall-walk. There are mural galleries with loopholes (two per arch) behind the arches. An upper wall-walk, presumably covered with a continuous breastwork (*epalxis*) with windows on the outside, ran along on top of the arches. The upper wall-walk was wide enough (*c.* 2.4m) to accommodate three-span catapults and leave enough space for their operation. The wall-walk of the mural gallery is nowhere wider than *c.* 1.6m, and narrows to *c.* 0.6m behind the buttresses. At best, the very small 1-cubit catapults could be emplaced there, with almost no room left for those tasked with serving these engines. Hence, there are two possibilities: either the

ABOVE LEFT
A mural gallery in an eastern curtain at Perge. The wall-walk is only *c.* 1.6m wide here and behind the buttresses it narrows down to *c.* 0.6m. There was not room enough for emplacing missile engines, so the mural gallery was either used only by archers, or else temporary wooden planking was emplaced beyond the stone wall-walk between the buttresses.

ABOVE RIGHT
The curtain on the western side of Perge, viewed from the city. Projecting courses of eaves are visible on its top. Rows of eaves allowed the widening of the wall-walk, thus making it more convenient for traffic and defence without conducting the labour-consuming work of broadening the entire wall.

D   GATES

(1A/1B) The main, East Gate of Priene, viewed from the outside and inside. Built in the 4th century BC, probably after 334, the gate was defended by two towers. The approach to it was via a *c.* 200 pace-long ramp next to the wall. Any assailants moving up this ramp presented an excellent target to the defenders. The next trap awaiting them lay behind the gate: on breaking through the latter, the assailants would find themselves in a small courtyard encircled by a crescent-shaped wall, from behind which the defenders brought fire to bear upon their right-hand side, which would not be protected by their shields. (2) The Main Gate of

Perge, late 3rd century BC. The gate is flanked by two formidable circular towers. The upper floors of the towers are adapted to house arrow-firing and stone-projecting devices. A postern was made in the outside of each tower, where it adjoins a curtain. The presence of posterns shows that the besieged were always ready to conduct an active defence, involving surprise sorties to attack the enemy. An oval-shaped courtyard behind the gate was designed to trap enemy soldiers, who could be destroyed easily there. (3) The Main Gate of Sillyon, with its two flanking towers. A semicircular wall beyond the towers forms a courtyard.

A curtain on the eastern side of Perge, viewed from the city. The wall is protected with buttresses ending with arches. A wall-walk wide enough to accommodate three-span catapults ran on top of the arches. A mural gallery was made between the outer wall and the arches, with two slits carved in each arch bay.

mural gallery was only used by archers, or temporary wooden planking was installed behind the stone wall-walk between the arches, allowing arrow-firing devices, up to three-span catapults, to be emplaced here.

The towers of Perge are rectangular (except those by the main gate), projecting in front of the curtain. On average, they are 13–14m high, 6–7m wide, and 8m deep. The wall-walk runs behind the towers. The towers mostly have three, but occasionally four, storeys. The bottom storey is usually (but not always) blind, the next storey features narrow slits, and there are large windows (c. 0.8m wide and c. 1.6m high) in the upper storey. The standard layout consists of three windows in each of the three projecting faces. Each tower could house at least one 5-mina stone-projector or several arrow-firing devices.

On entering the site, one finds oneself in front of a monumental Hellenistic main gate, which is flanked by two huge, round towers. Only half of each of them remains standing, but they are still very impressive. They were at least 18m high occupying a circle over 11m in diameter. The ground floor was blind, the first floor had slits, and the second and third floors had windows (two and

The main gate of Perge. The ruins of two round towers once flanking the gate can be seen in the foreground. Slits and windows for missile-throwing engines are visible in the ruined towers. There was an oval-shaped courtyard behind the gate.

eight respectively). Each of these towers could accommodate a considerable battery of arrow-firing devices as well as one or two stone-projectors. Between the windows of the upper storey were reliefs of circular shields – a common motif in Pamphylia, Pisidia and Lycia. The towers had conical, tiled roofs. Arched posterns were made on the outer (from the gate) sides of the towers. One such postern survives by the west tower. Behind the towers there was an oval courtyard, similar in shape to courtyards found at Sillyon and Side. Its rearward side probably narrowed between spurs, between which there was a second gate. The courtyard must have been built at the same time as the towers and gate. Early in the 2nd century AD a charitable citizen called Plancia Magna had it rebuilt, and statues of Roman emperors, as well as of Plancia Magna's relatives, were placed in the bays on the sides of the courtyard.

Side

Of all the Hellenistic fortifications at Side built some time between 225 and 188 BC, the land wall protecting the peninsula on the mainland is the best preserved. The fortifications along the shoreline, as well as the inner cross-wall, were rebuilt in a later period, and so will not be covered here.

Side is usually entered through the main gate. Two Hellenistic gates discovered in the city illustrate a characteristically Pamphylian concept of fortifications: a gate flanked by two towers with a courtyard at the rear where an enemy could be easily destroyed. Gates of a similar structure can be seen at Perge and Sillyon. Side, however, boasts a particularly powerful gate. Its two flanking rectangular towers do not stand a mere 20m apart from each other, leaving a narrow passage between them. There is also room, in the mouth of a semicircular courtyard, for a tower-like structure with a vaulted passageway (11m long and 7.25m wide) in the centre. The second storey of the structure was supposedly occupied by missile-throwing machines, which commanded the space in front of the gate. The exit from the semicircular courtyard behind the structure was intended to form a bottleneck. The latter was in fact another courtyard as tiny as 7.65m × 6.1m with an entrance as narrow as 3.3m and an only 3.55m-wide exit. Two more doors leading into the main courtyard made it possible for the defenders to attack the enemy on different sides. Unfortunately, only the traces of the foundations of the east side of this unique gate survive – the construction of a motorway in 1962 obliterated the remaining ancient ruins. The east gate differed from the main gate in having a rectangular courtyard and lacking either a central artillery structure or a second small courtyard. The main principles of construction were the same, though: the rear gate was narrower than the entrances and two more vaulted entrances were made on the sides of the courtyard. The lack of posterns in the land wall of Side indicates that the fortifications were not earmarked for active defence – the defenders relied upon firepower rather than sorties.

The best-preserved Hellenistic walls are on the left-hand side (facing the city) of the main gate. By walking along the walls on their inner side one can discover three types of curtain. Next to the gate is a section of a curtain backed by corbelled buttresses behind. The curtain is a solid 1.7m-thick wall here. A lower 3.4m-wide wall-walk runs on top of the buttresses. The short pillars of this wall-walk support the upper wall-walk.

Following the line of the walls, one will soon come across the second type of curtain. The upper floors are the same here, but the lower part of the wall has vaulting to the rear. Each arch, as does each interval between buttresses in

A section of a curtain backed by corbelled buttresses at Side. A slit has been made in each bay between the buttresses. Note that the slits are at different heights in different bays.

the first type, has *c.* 1m-long slits. Strange as it may seem, the slits do not widen out much towards the interior, thus allowing a very limited field of fire.

The third type of curtain also differs only in its lower part. Here the ground floor was solid and *c.* 3m wide. Three upper courses of eaves overhang at the rear to make the lower wall-walk broader. Slits in the lower part of a curtain of this type are much rarer than in the previous types.

A section of a curtain backed by arches at Side. A lower wall-walk was emplaced on top of the arches. The central slits in every bay between the pillars were designed for arrow-firing devices such as three-span catapults or even two-cubit engines. The small slit on the right-hand side was probably intended for an observer, who directed the artilleryman. The observer would find himself, however, in an extremely precarious and dangerous position being too close to the recoiling arm of any engine. The upper wall-walk and parapet are only preserved in fragments.

E THE CURTAINS AT SIDE

The fortifications at Side, which possibly date from a little later than those at Perge, were constructed with the same observance of the latter's main principle – to provide for maximum firepower. In Side, however, the architect was a creative professional: he devised three complex versions of the curtain, thus succeeding in obtaining an additional increase in their firepower. He may have experimented not knowing for certain which structure would turn out best. Whatever the case, the land wall acquired three types of curtain that differed in the structure of the lower part. In the first type, the lower part is a solid wall; the second type sees the wall backed by corbelled buttresses; in the third type the wall is fortified with arched buttresses. The upper part of all three

types of curtain is the same, and features two wall-walks. The parapet of the lower wall-walk was pierced by slits (two slits between pillars) while the continuous breastwork of the upper wall-walk had windows. Thus, the curtains in Side were provided with three tiers of fire (including the slits between buttresses). The lower wall-walk was evidently for arrow-firing devices (three-span catapults or even two-cubit engines). An arrow-firing machine shot through the central slit of each section of the wall. The right-hand slit was probably used by an observer, who directed the artilleryman. The observer's position must have been very uncomfortable and precarious because of the close proximity of the recoiling arm of any device.

Exterior and interior views of a tower by the East Gate at Side. The now missing upper floor possibly featured windows. The lower storeys in the towers at Side had only slits.

The upper sections were similar in all three types of curtain. The parapet of both the lower and upper wall-walk was *c.* 0.6m broad. In the lower wall-walk it was pierced with slits, two for each space between two pillars. It is curious that the left-hand slit (seen from the wall-walk) was of normal length, while the right-hand one was only half this size. Moreover, the longer slit is in the centre of the bay, whereas the shorter one is in a very awkward place, just by the right-hand pillar. The central slit seems to have been used for shooting an arrow-firing device (a three-span catapult or even a two-cubit machine, which could be accomodated on this wall-walk). The right-hand slit may have been used by an observer who directed the artilleryman, although the observer's position was dangerously close to the recoiling arm of the engine.

The structure of the parapet of the upper wall-walk has been much debated. Some scholars believe that there was a continuous breastwork (*epalxis*) with windows here, others think that there were battlements. Despite the fact that neither lintel-blocks nor coping-stones have yet been discovered, the first opinion prevails today.

The curtains were 11–12m high and 48.5–76m long (the distance between the towers). An unusual material – natural conglomerate, that is, rock consisting of individual stones that have become cemented together – was used in their construction. Marble insets can be seen occasionally interspersed in the wall.

Today one can see the ruins of 13 towers, of which 11 are rectangular (mostly about 10.7m x 9.5m tall), one is round, and the remaining one is half-round. As could be expected, the round tower stands at one of the most vulnerable places – at the north-west corner of the defences. The state of preservation of the towers at Side leaves much to be desired; moreover, some of the towers were rebuilt in the Byzantine period. Using the analogy of Perge's towers it can be presumed that those of Side rose another storey above the curtain. The upper storey may have had windows, while the lower ones had only slits. Entrance was by a door at ground level.

Most of the towers were brought completely forward of the curtain and connected with the curtains by two short walls (0.9–1.5m); each of the walls has a slit on the upper wall-walk level. This method of connecting towers and curtains served several purposes. First, the capacity of the towers to provide flanking fire was increased. Second, the collapse of a tower did not necessarily cause the collapse of the curtain, and vice versa. Third, a tower or a curtain could be isolated if it was seized by the enemy. For this purpose, easily removable wooden wall-walks must have been built beyond the towers.

Sillyon

The fortifications of Sillyon, built late in the 2nd century BC probably as a means of protection against Cilician pirates, differ dramatically from those of Perge and Side. While the latter both look impressively powerful and were designed to accommodate artillery, the fortifications of Sillyon are rather decorative. In some places the curtains are only one block thick (*c.* 0.6m), in other places they are two blocks thick (*c.* 1.2m). Sometimes the masonry is obviously ornamental, without any regard to function.

Sillyon comprised an acropolis and the lower city spreading uphill towards the acropolis. The fortifications of the lower town are comparatively well preserved. One can see the ruins of the main gate and a tower-gate. The entrance into a fortified street leading to the acropolis was protected by a small rectangular fort, sometimes called bastion D1.

The two surviving gates at Sillyon have different structures. The main gate is of a type widely used in Pamphylia: there are two towers on both sides of the gateway and a small courtyard formed by two semicircular walls behind the towers. The second surviving gate is a gate-tower consisting of a ground floor and two storeys. The gate proper is in the ground floor. It is curious that on the outer side the gate is overlapped by a lintel (a row of trapezoidal blocks, to be more exact) and on the inner side by a true arch. The wall-walk ran right through the tower, which is evidenced by the presence of doors on both sides of the tower. Small windows that can be seen on the first and second floors are clearly not meant for large stone-throwing devices, indicating that the weapons of the defenders of the tower consisted only of arrow-firing devices.

The unique fortified street leading towards the acropolis is a broad ramp about 5m across. There used to be two similar streets climbing towards the acropolis, on the northern and southern sides. Today the north road is heavily damaged, but the south street is in a much better condition. On the west it is protected by a defensive wall stabilized by buttresses for extra strength. Several merlons survive on the wall. Some scholars believe that the merlons were topped by wooden lintels to form windows, and that the whole of the fortified street was roofed. It seems unlikely, however, as in this case the defenders would be unable to shoot at the enemy in the street from the fort or the acropolis.

The fort (D1) adjoins a cliff that rises up to the acropolis. It is a small structure about 40m wide and 25m deep. There were two towers on its corners looking onto the street that led to the acropolis. One of them survives; the other collapsed and the breach was later filled with rubble and mortar masonry. Here and

A gate-tower at Sillyon. The wall-walk ran directly through the tower, evidenced by surviving doorways at the curtain-wall level. A fighting platform probably crowned the tower.

The southern fortified street leading to the acropolis at Sillyon. On the outside the wall is stabilized by buttresses for extra strength. Three surviving merlons are visible in the centre. The rectangular structure on the right is a fort, known as bastion D1, which protected the entrance to the street.

there the curtains of the fort stand to their full height (*c.* 8m) and are crowned with a wall-walk overhanging the inner side. The parapet is made from stone blocks only *c.* 0.85m in height, and it seems to have been this low in ancient times as well. This stone breastwork was probably crowned with wooden merlons or half-timber and half-mud-brick parapet. A doorway still exists in the north wall – it was possibly the only entrance to the fort.

Because of their thinness, the curtains are but poorly preserved – 12 courses at most, but rarely more than six. The wall-walk does not survive, but it was presumably made in the same way as the one in the fort: on stone blocks projecting on the inner side and balanced by the weight of a parapet.

The interior of the fort at Sillyon. The doorway in the north wall is the only entrance to the fort. The remains of a wall-walk overhanging the inner side are visible near the top of the walls. The parapet was made from stone blocks as little as *c.* 0.85m in height, and does not seem to have ever been of greater height than this. This stone breastwork was possibly crowned with wooden merlons or a half-timber and half-mud-brick parapet.

THE SITES AT WAR

The Greek fortified settlements in Asia Minor were seriously challenged for the first time by Lydian invasion. Early Lydian raids led by King Gyges against Greek *poleis* in the first half of the 7th century BC were unsuccessful. The Lydians were inexperienced in assailing fortifications and unprepared to lay down a long-lasting blockade of the cities. The same century witnessed the Cimmerians invading Greek coastal cities in Asia Minor. Ephesus was besieged and Magnesia on the Maeander was even destroyed, but, on the whole, these were bold forays, not proper subjugation; after sacking a city, the Cimmerians would withdraw. Faced with a threat of repeated Lydian and Cimmerian incursion, the Greeks had to restore their fortifications or replace them with more powerful ones in some places.

The next Lydian invasion was undertaken by Croesus in the mid-6th century BC. By that time the Lydians had mastered Near Eastern siege techniques, which many Greek urban fortifications could not withstand. Croesus seized some cities and imposed agreements on others. If before this invasion 'all Hellenes

The main gate at Perge, seen from the city side. The foreground is occupied by an oval-shaped courtyard. The wealthy citizen Plancia Magna had it rebuilt in the early 2nd century AD. Statues of Roman emperors as well as Plancia Magna's relatives were put in the recesses to the sides of the courtyard.

Over 900 balls of different calibres for stone-throwing engines were discovered in the acropolis of Pergamon, in the armoury built in the 3rd or 2nd century BC – clear evidence of the great number of such machines kept in supply by the city.

were free', according to Herodotus [1.6], they had to pay tribute to the Lydians now. On seizing a Greek city the Lydians destroyed its fortifications. As a consequence, in the second half of the 6th century BC many Ionians lived in settlements unprotected by walls.

Seeing Lydia routed by Cyrus the Great and facing the danger of Persian enslavement, the Ionians began to hurriedly encircle their cities with walls. It was to no avail, however; Harpagus, Cyrus' commander, took one Ionian city after another. He would surround a city with a rampart, make an embankment and seize the city by assault. Before starting a siege, Harpagus proposed that the citizens should pull down their fortifications in the most vulnerable place and acknowledge their loyalty to the Persian king. For instance, in Phokaia, which was the first Ionian city attacked by the Persians, Harpagus demanded that only one bastion be pulled down and one house in the city dedicated to the Persian king [Herodotus, 1.141, 1.162, 1.164].

In answer to the Persian challenge, Greek fortifications began to change later in the 6th century BC. The walls began to be sometimes preceded by a ditch – an extremely rare arrangement in the fortifications of the Archaic period. By the end of the century Greek walls were neatly laid of stone, gates were more formidable, and two-storey towers probably topped with an open fighting platform increased in number. City fortifications now usually consisted of the fortifications of the acropolis and outer city walls. All these innovations had first appeared in the Ionian settlements in Asia Minor, and only reached Greece proper one or two generations later. This degree of backwardness of the mother country was accounted for by its remoteness from Persia and consequently the less imminent threat of war in that period.

In 499 BC the Ionians rebelled against Persian oppression, but the rising was put down. Miletus, the last Greek city on the west coast of Anatolia, fell in 494 BC. Greek cities remained under Persian occupation for more than 150 years. The Ionian Revolt caused the Persian Wars (499–479 BC) with the result that the theatre of war was transferred to Greece. Her cities rushed to fortify themselves. Acquaintance with Near Eastern siege warfare forced the Greeks to revise their views of fortification and follow the example of their compatriots from Asia Minor. From that time on Greek defences featured carefully hewn masonry instead of the rubble seen in Archaic fortifications, a larger number of two-storey towers, and better-protected gates (now flanked by towers, or featuring a sharp bend – sometimes both). Moreover, mainland Greeks realized the danger of relying solely on a fortified acropolis. In most cities the whole built-up area was fortified now.

Dramatic changes in the Greek art of fortification took place in the 4th century BC, preconditioned by events in Sicily. In 405 BC Dionysius I became tyrant of Syracuse. With his lifelong military experience acquired in wars against Carthage, Dionysius I became the first Greek general who widely applied all the assortment of siege methods known and used by the Near Eastern empires. Not only did he actively use siege engines, but he also recruited mercenaries, mobilized manpower on a large scale, and resettled the inhabitants of occupied cities. Dionysius was also an innovator. His engineers are traditionally believed to have invented the prototype of a missile-throwing machine. In 399 BC, whilst preparing Syracuse for defence against a Carthaginian invasion, Dionysius invited the best engineers of Sicily, Italy and ancient Greece to come to the city. The combined efforts of the team were crowned with the birth of a new weapon based on a composite bow and given the name of *gastraphetes* ('belly bow'). In modern terminology it was a large crossbow that had to have one end laid on the ground while the other rested against the belly of the firer (hence the name) in order to string it. A *gastraphetes* was a very heavy weapon, so it was usually propped against a fortress wall or a hillock before firing. Its low rate of fire, compared with the ordinary bow, did not allow its active employment in field battles. The *gastraphetes* was mainly used in sieges and the defence of fortresses. In comparison with the ordinary bow the *gastraphetes* was much more powerful and had a longer range. Both these factors made a considerable impression on the enemy soldiers, who were not prepared for them.

The *gastraphetes* was first installed on a stand and supplied with a windlass around 375 BC. The resultant machine received the name of *oxybeles*. The first models of this engine shot bolts; soon, however, engines that launched small stone balls appeared. The balls were not heavy, though (about 2.25kg), so these engines were incapable of causing serious damage to fortifications and were only used as anti-personnel weapons.

Because of the limited possibilities of the composite bow, the power of this weapon could not be further increased. Therefore, engineers turned to another source of energy based on twisting thick cords of animal sinews, horse or human hair (women's hair was considered the best) soaked in oil. Such torsion-powered machines were not based around the bow but on an arm inserted into a rope bundle (torsion-spring). The torsion-springs were fastened to a wooden frame and twisted as far as possible by special levers at the top and at the bottom. Such arrow-firing machines with torsion-springs received the common name of catapult, meaning 'shield-breaker'. The machine is said to have been so powerful that an arrow fired from it could pass through a shield and an armoured warrior, standing behind it, at a distance of 400m. Torsion-powered machines were probably invented in Macedonia between 353 and 341 BC. Shortly afterwards, torsion-powered arrow-firing devices were adapted for casting stones. The Greeks called these stone-projectors *lithobolos*, the Romans *ballista*. The *lithobolos* was used for the first time by Alexander the Great at the siege of Halicarnassus in 334 BC. Here they were mainly employed against live targets. However, only two years later, at the siege of Tyre, these stone-projectors were already used for the destruction of fortifications – a task thoroughly beyond the power of an arrow-firer.

Recent discoveries have caused some researchers to date the invention of missile-throwing machines about two centuries earlier. A stone ball 29cm in diameter and weighing 22kg was discovered at Phokaia in the doorway destroyed in the Persian attack of 546 BC. A total of 422 limestone balls weighing for the most part between 2 and 12kg (some are as heavy as 21.8kg) were excavated from the ruins of the north-east gate of Old Paphos, dating from the Persian siege of the city in 498 BC. Surprisingly, these missiles have one flat side and resemble pieces of cheese. Later stone shots were ideally round in shape, leading some scholars to think the former belonged to the defenders and were launched by hand – one side was made flat so that they sat securely on the wall-walk or on the sill of an embrasure. However, unworked cobble-stones might be thrown by hand, too, while the labour-consuming operation of rounding off a boulder would only be worth the effort if aimed at improving the ballistic characteristics of missiles, which was necessary for balls fired by throwing engines. Pliny the Elder [*Natural History*, 7.201] asserts that it was the Cretans who invented the catapult, and Syro-Phoenicians were the authors of the ballista and the sling; his work was, of course, only a later compilation, though. It is also significant that the Persian garrison of Halicarnassus in 334 BC was equipped with arrow-firing devices. Certainly, the garrison included

The siege of Halicarnassus by Alexander the Great, 334 BC

a considerable detachment of Greek mercenaries, but on the whole this fact points to the appearance of missile-throwing engines in Asia Minor long before Alexander the Great. A supposition that they were invented in the 6th century or earlier by Phoenicians, Assyrians or Persians remains unproven. Even if throwing machines appeared before the 4th century BC, they were probably not very powerful and their influence on fortification was nil until that century.

How did the fortifications respond to the appearance of more aggressive siege warfare, and missile-throwing machines in particular? The subsequent changes were both strategic and tactical in character. With regard to the former, the layout and the location of defences as a whole, financial aspects that influenced the building of fortifications, and the strength of the defenders were all affected. The tactical changes comprised individual features of the fortifications that offered certain advantages to the defenders (for instance, the design of towers, curtains, gates, and so on).

The enclosing of all the hills and hillocks around the city with defensive walls was a strategic move. It gave two advantages to the defenders. First, it deprived the besiegers of commanding positions for their artillery. Second, placed on heights, the artillery of the defenders out-ranged that of the besiegers. Moreover, defenders could watch all the movements of the attacking troops.

ABOVE LEFT
The main gate at Perge, seen from the west. The photograph shows one of the two round towers beside the gate and the wall of an oval-shaped courtyard behind the gate. There is an arched postern at the side of the tower where a curtain once adjoined the tower. Posterns on the sides of towers enabled the defenders to make a surprise sortie and attack the enemy in the flanks or the rear.

ABOVE RIGHT
A rear view of a tower in the east wall at Perge. The second storeys of the towers at Perge were pierced by slits, while the upper storeys had large windows to allow stone-throwing machines to operate.

F   THE SIEGE OF HALICARNASSUS BY ALEXANDER THE GREAT, 334 BC

The events at Halicarnassus in 334 BC provide a demonstration of both an active siege and a no less active defence. It was the main naval base of the Persians in the southern Aegean, and the city was defended by a considerable Persian garrison and a large force of Greek mercenaries. Moreover, the Persians controlled the sea, and a fleet of triremes guarded the harbour. This seriously affected Alexander's position, as he had no siege engines at the beginning of the siege. Only some time later did his ships succeed in eluding the Persian fleet, allowing him to land his siege equipment at the bay near his camp. From that point onwards, Alexander's activity increased. The Macedonians filled up the ditch and began to prepare siege towers, ready to be moved closer to the walls. The defenders responded by making a night sally aimed at burning down the Greek siege machines. The sally was beaten off, but it made Alexander change his tactics. His sappers dug under the wall and brought down two towers and a curtain between them; a third tower was heavily damaged. The Macedonians were, however, too slow to profit from their success, as the besieged quickly raised a crescent-shaped brick wall beyond the fallen defences. The wall was fortified with a high wooden tower, which housed catapults (i.e., arrow-firing devices). Again Alexander ordered his siege engines to be moved to the wall, and again the defenders made a sally; this time they burned down their shelters and a siege tower. Alexander personally led the next assault, but in another sally the defenders attacked the Greeks on two sides; this moment is shown here. The Macedonians only just managed to beat them off. They probably owed much of their success to the torsion stone-projectors (*lithobolos*) mounted on wooden towers, which were used for the first time in this siege. Used here as antipersonnel weapons, these were probably only small experimental models, yet it only took two years to develop them into larger engines capable of damaging fortifications, as happened at Tyre. Having suffered great losses in this sally and fearful of an insurrection inside the city, the Persians withdrew from the city and confined themselves to the citadel. Alexander left a detachment to blockade the citadel, which held out for about a year, while he and his armies moved on.

This far-reaching circuit, known as 'the great circuit' or *Geländemauer*, was not invented in the 4th century BC. Its features can be found in the 14th/13th-century BC walls of Hattusha or some Greek cities of the 5th century BC. However, in Greek fortifications of the 4th and early 3rd centuries BC this old concept was revived and used more widely than ever before. Halicarnassus, Heracleia on Latmus and Ephesus can be cited as examples of 'the great circuits' in Asia Minor built between 370 and 270 BC. The disadvantage of 'the great circuit' was the excessive length of the defensive walls that encircled large uninhabited and unnecessary spaces. The construction of such long walls consumed huge amounts of labour and money. Moreover, a numerous garrison was needed to patrol and defend the walls. These two shortcomings would become clearly evident in the 3rd century BC and cause the replacement of 'the great circuit' by a more rational layout of the fortifications.

The tactical changes were no less significant. To counteract undermining, mobile towers and battering rams, the military architects of the 4th century BC set out a ditch in front of the city walls. Examples of this can be found at Athens (the Lycurgan walls), Megalopolis, Mantinea, and in Asia Minor at Halicarnassus. An alternative decision was to fortify a position on top of a hill with slopes too steep for siege machinery to be brought up and too rocky for undermining.

As for missile-throwing machines, because they were not powerful enough to destroy fortifications their use by besiegers was limited at first. But they found their place in the defences at once, and fortifications were soon adjusted for mounting these engines. They were originally placed only in towers, a natural choice, as towers in Greek fortifications were often roofed and curtains were usually not. Missile-throwing machines were, on the one hand, susceptible to the sun and rain (they could be completely ruined following exposure to rain) and, on the other hand, too heavy and unwieldy to be frequently transferred.

A characteristic feature of the artillery towers was wider slits or rectangular windows (unlike archers, who could shoot through ordinary slits, missile-throwing engines needed wider apertures). Artillery towers were also broader and longer than ordinary ones, as a machine would not just be mounted there but could be rotated. Early artillery towers, designed for non-torsion *oxybeles*, were probably built as early as the 370s or 360s BC. They certainly existed by the mid-4th century BC. By 340 BC torsion catapults began to be used in defence. The ground area of early artillery towers was generally between 50 and 100m². In Asia Minor such towers could be found at Alabanda, Alinda, Halicarnassus and Myndos.

According to Philon [I.27 and I.82], *lithoboloi* could easily bring a tower down and the use of these stone-projectors was among the simplest ways of seizing fortifications. Meanwhile, about a century before Philon, the siege of Tyre by Alexander the Great in 332 BC showed how ruinous torsion stone-projectors were for walls and towers. The maximum range of fire of a torsion throwing machine was 350–400m, but it had to be placed not further than 150–200m from the target in order to destroy a wall effectively. It was on the basis of this distance that Philon gave his recommendations on the organization of the defence [I.73].

To withstand a bombardment, fortifications were now to be much more strongly built. Special attention was paid to masonry design. It was discovered that bossed masonry better resisted the blows of battering rams and artillery bombardment, because the bosses protected the vulnerable joints between blocks from direct impact. However, the Greeks wished to see beautiful tooled faced masonry, which prevented this kind of masonry from becoming predominant.

Artillery towers of the second generation, which appeared after *c.* 325 BC, were generally bigger (their ground area was often over 100m²), thicker walled, had bigger windows, and their masonry was often very elaborate. These towers could be found at Cnidus, Ephesus, and Heracleia on Latmus.

Towards the late 4th century BC the defence of fortresses became active. The defenders no longer remained behind the walls, instead they made sallies to destroy the enemy siege weapons. In 334 BC at Halicarnassus and in 305–304 BC at Rhodes the sorties were numerous, and sometimes led to a real battle fought under the walls. By then the fortifications did not answer the needs of defence; there were few, if any, sally-ports at Halicarnassus so the defenders had to make sorties through a gate or a breach in the wall. Therefore, a great number of posterns were already made in fortifications built at the turn of the 4th/3rd centuries BC, as for instance, at Heracleia on Latmus or Ephesus.

In their attempt to adjust to more aggressive siegecraft, the fortifications themselves became more visually striking. Fortifications built in the late 4th century BC – for example, those at Colophon, Erythrae and Priene – carry notable stretches of *crémaillère* (jogs) providing for the enfilade of any approach routes. Moreover, half-round towers probably filled with rubble to the height of the wall-walks were built in numbers at Colophon. These towers must have been better able to withstand bombardment by missile-throwing machines.

However, despite all the efforts of the defenders and noticeable progress in the art of fortification, offence had gained the upper hand over defence by the end of the 4th century BC. An examination of the successive sieges and defences of Hellenistic cities made by A. W. McNicoll (1997, p. 47, and 1986, p. 310) shows that the art of siege reached its apogee in the very last years of the century. While between 322 and 318 BC only 46.2 per cent of sieges were successful, between 317 and 313 BC 62.1 per cent were so, between 312 and 308 BC 72.5 per cent were so, and between 307 and 303 BC out of a total of 21 sieges 20 were successful and only one was unsuccessful (Rhodes) – giving a percentage 95.2 per cent in favour of success. Almost no city could hope to survive an onslaught by the professional armies of Alexander's successors.

From *c.* 280 BC for about half a century Greek fortification was in a state of crisis. It is true that all the Greek cities in Asia Minor had been fortified by that time, but no noticeable modifications were made until *c.* 225 BC except that cross-walls (*diateichismata*) were built in some cities, which were, in the opinion of some scholars, designed to shorten the circuits in order to render the fortifications defensible by fewer men. An excellent example of such cross-walls is the *diateichisma* built at Heracleia on Latmus in the mid-3rd century BC that decreased the length of the walls from 6.5km to 4.5km. The crisis in fortification was caused by a lack of finance and a shortage of manpower. The wars of Alexander's successors and their descendants brought mainland Greece and Asia Minor to the point of complete exhaustion. The invasion of the Gauls only aggravated the situation. The cities became sorely impoverished and were unable to pay the cost of building fortifications and hiring mercenaries, while the successors' sponsorship had ended. In the 3rd century BC the strength of field armies was reduced, as well as the strength of garrisons, because the cities could no longer afford to hire strong detachments of mercenaries.

The 3rd century also saw a change in the tactics of siege warfare in Asia Minor. The offensive function of huge siege techniques of the late 4th century BC

The siege of Pergamon, 190 BC

was now carried on by small professional infantry detachments often equipped with nothing but scaling ladders. An assault was frequently simultaneous at different points around the defences, in order to split up the harassed defenders into even smaller groups. Early in the 3rd century BC the Romans had invented the famous *testudo* – a formation allowing soldiers not only to protect themselves with shields on their sides but also from above, so that they were completely protected from any missiles thrown at them. They first used the *testudo* in 293 BC at the siege of Aquilonia, where it was employed against a city gate that somebody had omitted to close in time. Soon they became so skilled in forming a *testudo* that they could easily overcome walls of moderate height with its help. By the end of the 3rd century BC the Romans had introduced the tactic of wearing down an enemy through continuous attacks; one wave followed another with fresh Roman detachments replacing the exhausted ones, thus depriving the defenders of a moment's rest. The Romans first tested this tactic at the siege of New Carthage in 209 BC,

G   THE SIEGE OF PERGAMON, 190 BC

The fortifications of Pergamon remained untested during the siege, but they played an important, though passive, role in its lifting. In 190 BC Seleucus IV, son of Antiochus III, ravaged the lands around Pergamon and forced the subjects of Eumenes II to seek sanctuary in the city. The besiegers camped almost at the foot of the hill. Nevertheless, reinforcements, consisting of 1,000 veteran Achaean infantry and 100 horsemen under the command of Diophanes, were successfully brought into the city at night. Two days later, seeing that the besiegers were playing games and drinking wine, Diophanes took his detachment out of the city gate and arrayed it beneath the wall. The enemy did not dare to attack them, probably for fear of coming under the fire from the city walls, and given that Diophanes' detachment was only small, the besiegers decided to continue having a good time. Diophanes waited until they had sat down for dinner and then ordered his men to charge, as shown in this illustration. The attack of the Achaean veterans was so swift and unexpected that the enemy had no time to pick up their weapons or mount their horses. Seleucus' people were routed and fled, despite their fourfold superiority. Numerous enemy troops were killed, and others were taken prisoner, before Diophanes' detachment made its triumphal return to the city. The next day saw the victorious troops exit the city once again and draw up under the protection of the city walls. This time the besiegers faced them in mirror formation – but did not dare to attack. They stood at the ready opposite each other for several hours until just before sunset, when Seleucus ordered a retreat to the camp. At that moment Diophanes suddenly attacked the enemy, destroying their rearguard before quickly returning to the protection of the walls. The Achaeans' bravery and audacity convinced Seleucus to lift the siege and withdraw.

then at the Spanish town of Orongis in 207 BC and the Aetolian town Heracleia in 191 BC.

It would be incorrect to say that the besiegers gave up using heavy siege engines and labour-consuming structures everywhere. The Romans had only mastered this technique by the mid-3rd century. For instance, besieging Lilybaeum in 250 BC, they built and used embankments, siege towers, battering rams and undermining. At the siege of Oreus in 200 BC they competed with King Attalus of Pergamon to be the first to take the city. According to Livy, 'as they attacked at different points, so they employed different methods. The Romans brought their *vineae* and battering rams close up to the wall, protecting themselves with their shield-roof; the king's troops poured in a hail of missiles from their *ballistae* and catapults of every description. They hurled huge pieces of rock, and constructed mines and made use of every expedient which they had found useful in the former siege' [Livy, 31.46.10]. The Romans won the competition: they were the first to penetrate into the town, after their battering ram had breached a part of the wall. This shows that Attalus' priority in artillery gave him no advantages. Although heavy siege technique was still widespread in Mediterranean countries, an assault was more often carried out by mobile storm units in the Near East and Greece in the 3rd century BC. Thus, Philip V resorted to embankments, undermining and missile-throwing machines whenever necessary, but preferred a surprise escalade by small professional infantry detachments. This tactic seems to have been developed by the rulers of the kingdoms of Macedonia and Syria.

The next stage in the evolution of the fortifications comes in the last quarter of the 3rd and the first half of the 2nd century BC, when military engineers were confronted with the following challenges: how to defend long, stretched-out defences with a small garrison, and how to build fortifications with scant means. The logical answering was giving up 'the great circuit' and building the shortest circuit possible. Shorter fortifications were cheaper and needed far fewer people to defend them. As a result, the walls became straight, or nearly straight, and only protected inhabited territory.

The need to make up for the lost advantages of higher ground, notably out-ranging the artillery of the besiegers, produced higher artillery towers. A new form of curtain was another tactical decision. Single-storey curtains began to be replaced with two- or three-storey ones (with two or three tiers of fire). Two wall-walks on these curtains allowed garrison troops to move more quickly from one place to another, while the greater height of a curtain made escalade more difficult. What was most important, however, was that these curtains permitted an increase in firepower, which combined with the small strength of a garrison led to a return to passivity in defence (risking the few defenders' lives in sallies could hardly be justified). The necessity of increasing firepower added significance to light anti-personnel artillery in the late 3rd century BC. It was then that Philon [*Bel.*, 73.21–77.8.] described a newly invented repeating catapult (*polybolos*). The ability of the engine to fire automatically until the bolts ran out was especially useful in defending fortifications. Although it fired too many missiles in one place, the machine was probably highly effective in repulsing an assault.

Two more tactical principles that appeared in this period are worth mentioning. With the move from active to passive defence the importance of ditches grew, while that of posterns decreased. Complex gateways, with courtyards where the enemy could be destroyed after they had broken through the outer fortifications, also became popular.

The fortifications of Perge and Side are excellent examples of the application of the new strategic concepts and the new tactical methods.

However, the structure of the mainland wall of Iasus, dating from the turn of the 3rd to the 2nd century BC, goes against the above-described tendencies. The low artillery walls and towers, the absence of a ditch, and the numerous sally-ports all bear witness to the fact that active defence was relied upon. The relief of the terrain did not allow the enemy to bring up heavy siege engines. Therefore, in contrast to adopted Hellenistic practice the object of the sallies in this case was not the destruction of *matériel* but the annihilation of the enemy. Deceived by low walls and towers, the enemy would rush to the attack without preparation – and would be bombarded with missiles from numerous engines while still far from the walls. Any of the battered enemy that reached the fortifications would be attacked on both sides from numerous sally-ports. The structure of the Iasus mainland wall is unique and should be examined apart from the urban fortifications. Erected by the field army of Philip V of Macedon, the wall was to be defended by the same army. There was thus no question of a shortage in manpower, and this explains why the structure of the wall served a different tactical purpose to other urban fortifications of the time.

The above-mentioned trends in the evolution of fortification under the influence of siege warfare should by no means be considered as absolute. They were no more than general tendencies. The building of fortifications was affected by numerous factors, economic ones being the most important. Not every city could afford to enclose all the high ground around it. In Erythrae, for instance, a ridge towered over the south wall, so it was decided to erect a very thick wall (up to 5.2m in places) there, nearly twice as thick as the usual Hellenistic wall in the area. Missile-throwing machines were expensive and professionals were needed to build them. A lack of financial means often prevented a city from buying such engines or hiring skilled engineers. Hence, the fortifications of these cities had few towers, or the towers were not spacious enough to accommodate artillery (as at Priene, Myndos and Caunos).

Even rich cities often considered it inexpedient to have powerful fortifications built all along the perimeter. For instance, it was not worthwhile to erect thick, multi-level curtains and large artillery towers at places where the terrain offered excellent protection (along the edge of a steep precipice, for example) and excluded any possibility of siege engines being brought close to the wall. Gates required the most protection, as they allowed the approach of wheeled traffic, as did walls bordering open country or water deep enough to sail in. Heavy siege machines could easily approach the defences in these areas, and so towers carrying powerful stone-throwing devices capable of destroying enemy engines or demolishing their siege-towers and tortoises would expect to be sited here. According to Philon [IV.17, III.67–68], the destruction of missile-throwing engines could be done by 10-mina stone-throwers (with an approximate size of 6.4 x 3.2m), while the breaking of siege-towers required 30-mina stone-throwers (approximately 9.2–4.6m). The latter could only be mounted – with difficulty – in very large towers (with a footprint of over 100m²).

Cities such as Pednelissus and Sillyon are exceptions to the rule. Their fortifications were too weak to stand up to an army supplied with siege engines. Their fortifications are usually linked to the time of the Roman protectorate (after 133 BC). Whether Rome forbade them from building strong defences, or the cities believed their security guaranteed, the walls of Pednelissus and Sillyon could only protect their citizens from pirates and robber gangs, which periodically appeared in southern Asia Minor.

A U-shaped tower at Assos. Dating from the late 3rd century BC, the tower afforded space for artillery pieces. On its single floor there was possibly an arrow-firing device that was moved from one window to another with the help of a system of pulleys.

OPPOSITE TOP
The south cross-wall at Miletus is an excellent example of how far the art of fortification had advanced by the end of the period in question. It was built in the late 2nd/1st century BC, that is, shortly after the city had been annexed by Rome. The wall provides evidence of the most extensive defensive activity ever undertaken in ancient Asia Minor. The only other example of such 'offensive' defence is to be found in the Iasus mainland wall, which served, however, to protect a military camp. The fortifications of Perge and Side, although designed to accommodate greater firepower, are passive on the whole, featuring only a few posterns. The south cross-wall at Miletus comprised heavily projecting rectangular towers, with posterns flanking every tower, and straight curtains connecting the towers. Some of the curtains were abnormal, having engine stores in special arched bays at ground level. The towers provided powerful flanking fire. The entire system, and the absence of any moat in front of the fortifications, shows that an active defence was relied upon. Unfortunately, these fortifications are barely visible today – having been excavated, they were almost completely buried again. (After Gerkan and Wiegand)

First-rate fortifications, with large artillery towers and multi-level curtains, were usually the privilege of strategically important cities, notably those sponsored by the rulers of strong kingdoms. Autonomous cities, with perhaps the exception of Rhodes, could not afford such fortifications. Medium-sized cities such as Side or Perge built second-rate fortifications with sophisticated multi-level curtains, but with towers only large enough for small-calibre artillery. Poorer cities could only afford third-rate fortifications consisting of plain curtains and small towers sometimes unfit for mounting any artillery. Consequently, many cities could only withstand a medium- or low-level attack. Whatever the level of the development of the art of fortification, such cities could never oppose large armies equipped with siege engines.

The impact of economic factors on the state of fortification can clearly be seen in the city of Assos. Its 4th-century fortifications, although not designed for mounting artillery, had numerous sally-ports and gates. It means that the city was under royal patronage and had a large body of professional mercenaries for its protection. In the early 3rd century BC the city probably became independent. The citizens could no longer afford to man extensive fortifications and had to build cross-walls (*diateichisma*). In 241 BC the city came under Pergamene hegemony and could count on royal resources. As a result, in the late 3rd century BC its fortifications were modernized and received a formidable U-shaped artillery tower.

AFTERMATH

Most of the Greek cites in Asia Minor continued to survive under Roman rule, and some even prospered more than before. The Romans brought their habitual structures and entertainment to Greek cities, which now acquired aqueducts, baths and other public buildings. Amphitheatres, however, never became popular in Greece and Asia Minor and gladiatorial combats were instead held in theatres and stadiums. Under the Romans city defensive walls in Asia Minor acquired a more symbolic rather than military significance, functioning as a demarcating line. Those built by the Romans were weak and thin, as the Romans apparently relied on their field army more than on fortifications. They paid special attention to the gate, though; many gates rebuilt in this period lost their severe appearance and acquired a more ceremonial one. A gate

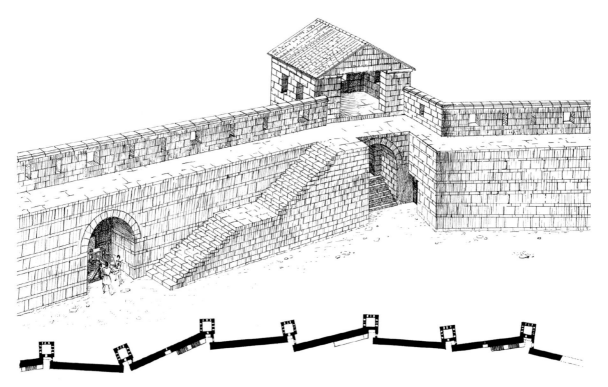

and a forum were often connected by a colonnaded street, which formed a comfortable walking and shopping area. Perge and Side offer examples of such modifications. In the early 2nd century AD a rich citizen called Plancia Magna restored and embellished with statues the courtyard of the main gate in Perge; the 3rd century AD saw a decorative, so-called Roman gate grow before the main Hellenistic gate. A similar situation was observed at Side. About 200 AD, when military needs diminished, the courtyard by the main gate was adorned with pillars, niches and statues. Colonnaded streets stretched from the gate to the centre in both cities.

The Middle Ages saw some cities abandoned. In others, the fortifications were considerably reconstructed. Unable to defend long ancient walls, the Byzantines or Seljuqs erected a smaller citadel inside the old city. Some re-used material can often be seen in the walls (fragments of columns, and gravestones) and a medieval wall can occasionally be seen built on the foundations of ancient walls. However, medieval walls were never laid the way the ancient Greeks did. It is impossible to confuse the rubble-cum-mortar of a medieval wall with the accurate masonry of well-adjusted dry blocks characteristic of ancient Greek fortification.

BELOW LEFT
This so-called Roman gate at Perge was probably built in the 3rd century AD right in front of a monumental Hellenistic gate. An additional line of fortifications built to the south was seemingly designed to protect the expanded territory of the city. Meanwhile, the Roman fortifications were far from formidable, and were probably only created for effect.

BELOW RIGHT
A medieval tower in the acropolis at Assos. In the Byzantine and Turkish periods the ancient fortifications of Assos were rebuilt. The masonry of medieval towers, often erected on ancient foundations, was quite different, consisting of rubble on mortar.

Over the ensuing centuries ancient Greek fortifications were picked apart by people from neighbouring villages, who used the neatly hewn stone blocks for their domestic needs. This happened both in the Middle Ages and relatively recently. For instance, as late as the 18th and 19th centuries the ruins at Assos were counted among the finest Hellenic remains anywhere. But the site suffered considerable damage in the second half of 19th century as it was used as a quarry for builders in Istanbul. The ancient walls and the theatre, as well as the main gate that until then had survived almost intact, suffered irreparable damage. A similar fate befell Iasus. The defensive wall once surrounding the city on the peninsula was also seriously destroyed when it was used as a quarry for the Bebek jetty in Istanbul in 1889. The destruction was so complete that the researchers visiting the site in 1954, before archaeological excavation had started, discovered no remains of the Hellenic or Hellenistic wall. Even today, after all the excavation, the Greek fortifications are extremely difficult to make out, and plans are usually drawn on the basis of sketches and drawings made before 1889.

THE SITES TODAY

Alabanda (Caria)

Near Doganyurt (Araphisar), about 5km from Çine. What remains of the fortifications of Alabanda, already extant in the 3rd century BC and probably built a century earlier, can hardly be described as 'preserved'. They consisted of 30 towers – 28 rectangular, one pentagonal and one round – interrupting the walls every 45–98m. Today most of them lie in ruins; only three towers in the south wall (nos. 2, 3 and 4) are about half as high as they used to be. The pentagonal tower (no. 23) looks like the combined halves of two rectangular towers so as to form five irregular sides. Nothing but the foundation survives of the round tower (no. 7), which seems to have stood apart from the wall and was unconnected with the latter.

Alinda (Caria)

The ruins lie on two hills above the village of Karpuzlu, some 50km to the south of Aydin. The defensive walls were supposedly built in the 4th century BC, certainly before *c*. 340. The fortifications comprise an acropolis, and city walls running down the hills. About 1,400m of the defensive walls survive. Rectangular towers are distributed more or less evenly along the walls. Out of the 19 surviving the nos. 1 and 7 towers rise nearly to their original height. Ten towers out of the 19 belong to the acropolis. Zig-zagging wall projections replace towers on the north and south sides of the acropolis. On the east side, nothing remains of the outer acropolis fortifications or the city walls. It remains unclear how the inner perimeter of the acropolis was connected with the outer as no traces of an entrance gate have been found.

Amos (Caria)

Near Turunç village, not far from Marmaris. The best-preserved section of the wall with its five towers runs along the slope of a hill, parallel to the sea. Besides, there is another massive wall at the west end of the site, near the temple and beyond the main defence line. Some remains of the walls can also be seen to the south-east of the temple. Screened now by thickets of trees and bushes, the walls are hardly noticeable from afar. However, the fortifications still reach as high as 7–8m in places. They are built of polygonal masonry occasionally

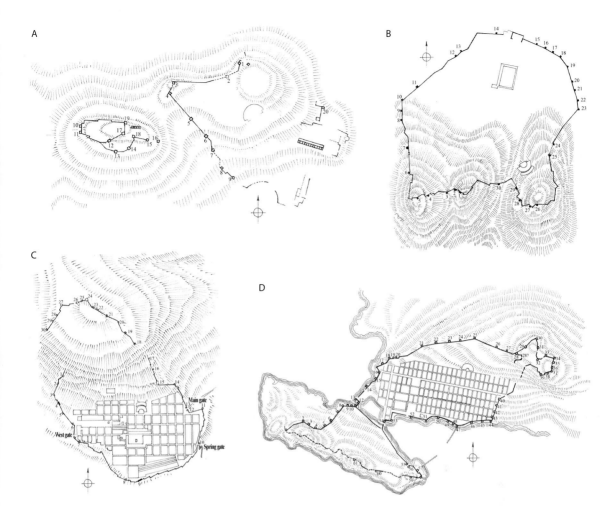

A

B

C

D

topped by rows of irregular ashlar. The latter masonry is supposed to have appeared as a result of later repair of the original walls probably erected early in the 4th century BC. A strange combination of a projecting wall and access steps can be seen to the east of the gate by the no. 4 tower. A large window in the curtain 11m east of tower no. 2 is another curiosity of the fortifications of Amos. It was supposedly used for bombarding the beach to hinder enemy landings. The window would thus be a result of later repairs done in the artillery age.

Several plans of fortifications.
A: Alinda (after McNicoll).
B: Alabanda (after McNicoll).
C: Priene (after Wiegand and Schrader). D: Cnidus (after Gerkan and McNicoll).

Assos (Troad)

Near modern Behram (Behramkale) village, about 20km south-west of Ayvacik. Assos fortifications date from more than one period. The most ancient ones, erected in the polygonal/Lesbian masonry style, may have been Lydian. They were rebuilt in the 4th century BC, but before the spread of torsion artillery. The early 3rd century BC saw the construction of a cross-wall (*diateichisma*) and at the end of the same century, probably under Pergamene hegemony, the fortifications were modernized, particularly in the north-west section. It was at that time that a semicircular tower, for mounting artillery, was erected. Finally, many towers of the acropolis were rebuilt in the Middle Ages, during the Byzantine and Turkish periods. Ancient Greek fortifications have been best preserved in the lower town. Here the visitor's eye is caught by the ruins of the

The fortifications of Assos dating from the Hellenistic period. In the centre of the photograph there is a postern next to a rectangular tower.

impressive, main West Gate as well as numerous towers. The main gate was flanked with two powerful rectangular towers with a passage between them under a lintel crowned with false pointed arches at both ends. The passage led into a small rectangular courtyard (9.6 × 6.2m) with a guardhouse (3.10m²) on its east side. The most interesting is the semicircular, or rather, U-shaped tower. Erected in the age of artillery, it has only one floor, at mid-height, where there are five windows. The windows look wide enough on the outside, but owing to their hourglass form in plan, the apertures inside the wall are no more than 0.2m wide. This is why the windows could be used by arrow-firing devices, but not by stone-projectors. The tower's peculiar feature was two pairs of corbels fastened at the top of the inside flanking walls above the apertures, as well as a stone ring (now reduced to a stump) above the aperture at the front of the tower. The devices were possibly needed to fasten the system of pulleys necessary for turning a catapult to face a different slit. A supposition that the tower had another floor, one with larger windows for placing stone-throwing engines, seems unlikely.

Cadyanda (Lycia)

Near Üzümlü, about 20km from Fethiye. The fortifications dating from the late 3rd–2nd century BC survive on a small site on the south-west side of the city. Here the wall rises over 8m to the wall-walk. It is interesting that the curtain is backed at intervals of 4.2m by buttresses as thick as the walls (1.2m). The masonry of the curtains is principally different from that of the buttresses (uncoursed polygonal and coursed ashlar), but as these buttresses are bonded into the wall there is little doubt that they are contemporary. A wooden wall-walk may have existed on the buttresses.

BELOW LEFT
Persikon hill, home to the acropolis of Caunos. The walls, built from rubble on mortar, were added in the Middle Ages onto the ancient foundations.

BELOW RIGHT
A tower at Canytelis/Kanytelleis. Each floor was partitioned into three living rooms. The only surviving entrance is on the ground floor.

Caunos/Caunus/Kaunos (Caria)

Near modern Dalyan, about 15km west of Ortaca. The fortifications of Caunos stretch over two hills, Persikon and Herakleion, and enclose the ancient harbour lying between them. Persikon, or the acropolis, was the first to be fortified, in the 6th or 5th century BC. The first city defences, not yet extensive, date from the late 5th or early 4th century BC (before 394 BC). In the middle of or towards the end of the 4th century BC (but before 309 BC) fortifications appeared on Herakleion. The 3rd or 2nd century BC may have seen walls at some sections repaired and a few towers added. All these stages are reflected in the styles of masonry that vary from polygonal/Lesbian to uncoursed or coursed ashlar. The rubble and mortar walls on the acropolis (Persikon) appeared in the Middle Ages. Among the six ancient towers, tower T6 with its middle floor pierced by slits is best preserved. The towers vary from small (*c.* 5 × 5m) to large (*c.* 14 × 11m). In two places in the section H–J, the curtains survive at their full height (7–8m), merlons included. Both the merlons and the crenels between them are *c.* 1.6m long each. Each merlon has a *c.* 0.45m² projection on its left side and two grooves. The latter may have served to fasten shutters or for a kind of a mechanism that pushed scaling ladders away.

Canytelis/Kanytelleis/Kanlidivane (Cilikia)

About 30km east of Silifke. A detached tower at Canytelis, like the tower at Diocaesarea, is a good example of a private residential tower (*tyrsis*). Dating from *c.* 200 BC, it is rectangular (15 × 9m) with 1.4m thick outer walls. Each of the three surviving floors was partitioned into three rooms. The only surviving narrow entrance with a relieving arch over the lintel is on the ground floor. Each floor was pierced by loopholes.

Cnidus/Knidos (Caria)

Near Yazi village, at the end of the Datça peninsula. The fortifications at Cnidus, supposedly dating from *c.* 330 BC, protected two large areas: the mainland, where an acropolis commanded the city from the top of a hill, and a part of the adjoining peninsula. Two harbours were fitted between these fortified grounds: a military one, the smaller of the two, and a commercial one. The military harbour was integrated into the defences: it was enclosed in the fortified city area and could only be entered through a passage little wider than a common gate. The defences of the commercial harbour were considerably less substantial, probably owing to its size. Nevertheless, the walls with towers running along the shores allowed precision fire to be brought to bear upon the whole of the harbour; 400m wide at the widest points, it could be covered with fire from torsion arrow-firing devices. The curtains and towers have retained half of their original height, at best. Out of 61 towers discovered to date, most are rectangular and two are semicircular in shape. The latter, protecting the entrance to the military harbour, may have been added later, possibly in the 2nd century BC.

Colophon (Ionia)

Near modern Degirmendere, about 20km south of Izmir. The east part of what were once more than 4km-long perimeter walls has been best preserved but even here the fortifications are ruined and so overgrown that they are hard to reach. The wall running down the hill in the north-east section is fortified with towers, while the wall on the south-east has jogs instead of towers. An indented

A tower at Diocaesarea, viewed from the east. Two doors have been discovered in the tower: one on the ground floor (in the southern wall), the other on the second floor (in the eastern wall). The designation of the latter is subject to debate. Some scholars believe that it was a second entrance to the tower, others think that it opened onto a balcony and was made solely for amenity. The fact that the door leads to a stone staircase connecting the storeys, not to a room, seems to lend weight to the former interpretation.

trace here is well founded, as from the indents the unprotected right-hand side of the assailants could be covered with strong enfilade, while a tower protected the upper projection from a frontal attack. The frequent use of semicircular towers (nine out of the surviving 14) is a characteristic feature of the fortifications at Colophon.

Diocaesarea (Cilicia)

Modern Uzuncaburç ('Tall Tower'), about 30km north of Silifke. The Hellenistic tower in Olba, better known by the Roman name Diocaesarea, is another example of a *tyrsis* or private residential tower. The six-storey tower was supposedly erected in the 3rd century BC. Each of its three lower storeys contained five rooms, and each of the three upper ones four. Communication between the storeys was by a stone staircase. The tower is 15.6×12.5m in plan. The walls were 1.2m thick at the bottom and *c.* 1m thick at the top. Two entrances lead into the tower – one on the ground floor (in the south wall) and the other on the second floor (in the east wall). Hourglass-shaped slits have been preserved on the first, second and third floors. The slits of the third floor differ in structure from those made below. The latter seem to have been cut some time after the tower was built, as they were made in a course and a half of blocks, which is unusual.

Ephesus (Ionia)

About 3km from modern Selçuk. The over 9km-long defensive walls encircling the city were raised by Lysimachus in *c.* 290 BC. A considerable section of them has been preserved. It lies, however, far from the tourist track, on the almost inaccessible hill of Bülbüldagi. Only separate fragments of a Hellenistic circuit, as well as later Byzantine walls, are visible at ground level. In some places the Hellenistic walls survive at almost full height (6.5m) up to the wall-walk. They were supposedly crenellated with a merloned parapet, which would increase the height of the curtain to *c.* 8.5m. Researchers have counted between 42 and 48 surviving towers and 16 posterns. The towers differ appreciably in size – from *c.* 7×7m to *c.* 15×15m. Two big towers partitioned into rooms (one into three rooms, the other into four) are of the latter size. These towers were evidently used as barracks for the garrison as well. All the towers were two-storeyed, probably gabled and roofed with tiles. The wall-walk usually ran behind the towers. Both slits and also engine windows (*c.* 2m high and 1.2–0.7m wide, narrowing on the outside) have been preserved in some of the towers.

Within sight of Ephesus there is a Hellenistic hilltop fort that probably served as an observation and signalling station. The fort is square with 25m-long sides. Instead of towers the fort has three-sided rectangular partial salients on the corners.

Erythrae (Ionia)

Located 22km north-east of modern Çesme and built between 330 and 315 BC, the city walls of Erythrae are poorly preserved. Most of them were destroyed in the 19th century when they were used as quarries. A curious feature of the walls is alternate courses of red trachyte and white limestone. Only four towers survive, and only on the basement level, all of them on the south-east side of the perimeter.

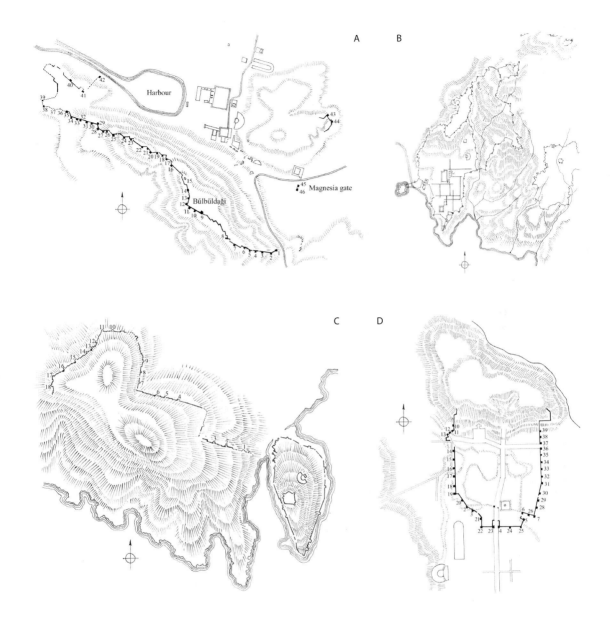

Forts in Caria

A number of sentry and signal posts were discovered in Caria: Teke Kale, At Yaylasi (Attau-lu-su), Kurun Dere, Bagacik (Baghajik), Ören (Euren), Altin Tas (Altyn Tash) and Labraunda. Teke Kale is a fort with a square tower (11.5 × 11.5m in plan) and *c.* 230m-long walls forming inner and outer courtyards. Barracks for a garrison, supposedly 64 men strong, adjoin to the walls. Fortifications at Yaylasi comprise an enclosed area and tower. Kurun Dere was a small fort on a high spur of Grion commanding the road from Miletos and Heracleia to Mylasa. Difficult to access, Fort Bagacik sits on a crest above the valley of Latmus. The natural strength of the place was fortified with walls, which survive in some places. Ören and Altin Tas resemble Bagacik. They are as hard to reach as the latter, but the fortifications of Ören consist of two lines of walls, outer and inner. The three kinds of fortification discovered in Labraunda were probably also used to keep watch. One of them (the so-called Tepe Hisar Kale) is a tower (11.8 × 11.8m in plan),

Several plans of fortifications. A: Ephesus (after Benddorf and McNicoll). B: Heracleia on Latmus (after Krischen and Lyncker). C: Iasus (after Judeich and McNicoll). D: Perge (after Lanckoronski).

53

divided into four rooms, with ruined walls adjoining the tower. A slim stronghold, Burgas Kale, sits on another hill. The third one, known as the 'acropolis' of Labraunda or Hisar Kale, is a fort irregular in plan, with walls about 400m long in perimeter and featuring projecting towers.

Halicarnassus (Caria)
Modern Bodrum. The walls erected by Mausolus in the mid-4th century BC stretched for over 6.5km. Today they can be traced for about 5.5km. Researchers number from 18 to 27 towers, but most of them lie in ruins now. The fortifications of the Myndos Gate are best preserved. The gate was strengthened with two towers, one of which is still about 7m high. There is a 7m-wide and 2.5m-deep ditch in front of the gate.

Heracleia on Latmus (Caria/Ionia)
The magnificent ruins of this site lie near the village of Kapikiri, on the eastern shore of Lake Bafa. In places the fortifications chiefly dating from *c.* 300 BC (the great circuit, or Heracleia I) are very well preserved. The *diateichisma* or cross-wall (Heracleia II) was built in the mid-3rd century BC or later. The curtain, which rises to a maximum height of 5.8m, was crowned with a continuous breastwork (*epalxis*) from 2.25 to 3.25m high and *c.* 0.85m wide, with occasional loopholes. The walls of the great circuit, stretching for 6.5km, feature 65 towers; a further 50 towers strengthen the *diateichisma* and the lower citadel (4.5km). The towers are rectangular, semicircular and with curved faces. The rectangular towers are more characteristic of Heracleia I, while the semicircular and those with curved faces relate to Heracleia II (comprising 20 per cent of all the towers here). Most of the towers are two storeys high, and three-storeyed ones are rare. Slits for archers are common in the walls of the lower storey, while the upper storey has windows for throwing engines.

Iasus (Caria)
Near Kiyikislacik village, about 30km west of Milas. The city occupied a small peninsula, where a medieval (possibly Byzantine) fortress can be seen today. The ancient Greek city wall of the 4th century BC that followed the outline of the peninsula is hardly visible. Most interesting, however, is a well-preserved section of the mainland wall. For a long time the dating of the fortifications was a point of debate. Today, A. W. McNicoll's supposition [1997, pp. 115–17] that they were built by the army of Philip V of Macedonia blockaded at Caria at the turn of the

Heracleia on Latmus. The magnificent ruins of the Hellenistic fortifications have been preserved here and there on a ridge of the rocks towering over Lake Bafa.

3rd and 2nd centuries BC appears most probable. In this case they were fortifications of a military camp, not urban fortifications. The surviving section of the mainland wall is about 3km long and up to 5.5m high. Some 18 towers were placed along the wall at a distance of between 50 and 200m (that is, within the range of accurate bowshot and a low-trajectory engine). All towers are semicircular but have straight sides and a rounded front face (so they are U-shaped rather than D-shaped). They jut out 9–17m. The curtains beyond them stretched in an unbroken line. The towers are open on the gorge and are the same height as the curtains. There is a sally-port in each tower-flank, immediately by the curtain. Five windows were made about 3m above the present outside ground level in the bottom storey in the front part of each tower. The towers were topped by a fighting platform, which was probably crenellated. Besides the towers, the possibility of enfilade fire was provided by 32 jogs, generally about 3.8m deep, each with a postern and slot. The jogs were usually made in such a way that the unprotected right-hand side of the assailants could be attacked. About every 30m a curtain was interspersed with either a tower or a jog. Numerous vertical slits as long as 50–60cm can be seen by the main gate and along the curtains. These slits were designed for arrow-firing devices and correspond to the *scorpio*-slits for Syracuse described by Livy [24.34.9].

Loryma (Caria)

Loryma fortress is situated at the very end of the Karaburun peninsula, near Bozukkale, about 50km south-west of Marmaris. The site is rather hard to reach; the journey involves a sea trip to Bozukkale Harbour followed by more than an hour's walk or another sea trip in a hired boat. There are three Lorymas known to us. The earlier forts Loryma I and II are to be seen 2–3km inland. They served as a refuge against marauders. Loryma III is the best known of the three. Built in the 3rd or 2nd century BC to defend the harbour, it was more than a simple refuge. The fortress of Loryma III stretches for 324m, but is only 30m wide. Two round towers stand at the extreme points of this stretch of land, with nine rectangular towers placed along the walls between them. All the towers are small, and are among the smallest of all the Hellenistic towers. There is a 1.6m-wide window in the westernmost rectangular tower; in the other towers only slits have been preserved. Five posterns were cut in the walls, each of them beside a tower. The fortifications were made using huge stone blocks up to 4m long and an average of 0.6m in height.

A reconstruction of the mainland wall at Iasus. The wall was interspersed at about 30m with jogs or U-shaped towers, allowing them to enfilade the enemy effectively. Moreover, there were sally-ports on either side of every tower and at every jog. Numerous posterns made an active defence possible, with surprise sorties by the defenders. The wall was laid with uncoursed rubble, which is uncharacteristic of Greek military architecture.

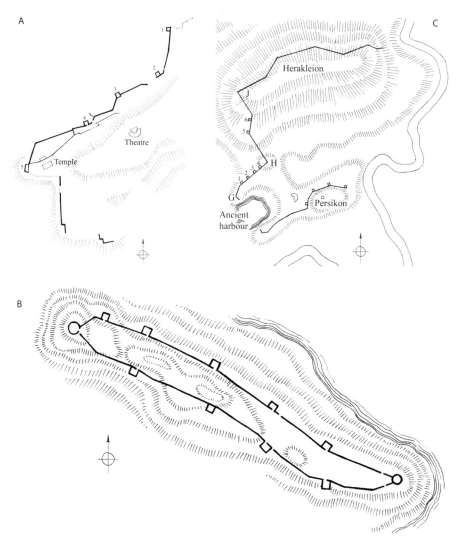

Several plans of fortifications.
A: Amos (after McNicoll).
B: Loryma (after Niemann).
C: Caunos (after Bean and McNicoll).

The Myndos Gate is the only surviving gate at Halicarnassus. Like other fortification work there, the gate was built in the mid-4th century BC by Mausolus, satrap of Caria, who obtained considerable independence from Persia.

Myndos (Caria)

Near modern Gümüslük on the western tip of the Bodrum peninsula, about 20km from Bodrum. The half-destroyed walls have been preserved in some places together with a tower as high as six courses of masonry. The fortifications were built some time between 367 and 334 BC.

Myra (Lycia)

About 1km west of the village of Beymelek, not far from modern Demre (Kale), lies the fort known as the Myra East Fort or Isium. The fort comprises two square towers (with a 5.75m-long side) connected by a 0.75m-wide curtain so as to form a small irregular courtyard. The entrance is in a salient formed by a bend in the walls. The curtains had two to three storeys (depending on the terrain), while the towers were four-storeyed. The wall-walk along the curtains was built from wooden planking put on joists, which in turn were placed on a splayed cantilevered course. Slits and windows were provided in the towers and curtains. Both the towers and a considerable part of a curtain on the south side have been fairly well preserved.

West of the Demre Valley and on the opposite side of the River Demre stands a solitary tower. It is sometimes called the Myra West Fort, though the word 'fort' is perhaps not the best term to apply to this solitary tower. Opinions differ as to its purpose. Some believe it was a signal-watch tower, but considering its inner plan and its likeness to similar towers in Canytelis and Diocaesarea, it should rather be acknowledged as a fortified residence (tyrsis) of some Lycian potentate.

A reconstruction of the Myra East Fort or Isium (after McNicoll). The fort comprises two square towers connected by curtains in such a way as to form a small irregular courtyard. The entrance to the fort is in a salient made by a bend in the walls. The curtains were two to three storeys high (depending on the terrain), and the towers had four storeys.

Erected probably in the 2nd century BC, like the Myra East Fort, the tower is 14.4 × 12m in size. Once it had three storeys under a gabled roof; the entrance was on the ground floor. Each storey was partitioned into three rooms. Each, except the lower one, had windows provided with shutters. Irregular holes, which can be seen in each face just below the course that carried the first floor, were possibly used for ventilating the ground floor. The tower is also supplied with drains, which, considering there was a roof, may have been used for throwing out slop and sewage. About 25m east of the tower there are two rock-cut cisterns. The most curious feature of the tower is probably two corbels, half a metre apart, overhanging the entrance. If they served as the bases for machicolation, then this is the only known instance of machicolations in Greek military architecture to date.

Oenoanda (Lycia)

Above the village of Incealiler, about 50km east of Fethiye. Of the fortifications dating from between 188 and 159 BC a small section of the south wall with two towers, one pentagonal and one round, is best preserved. The curtains rise up as high as the wall-walk (c. 6m). The wall-walk is formed by two courses of eaves, projecting at the rear. Only the foundation of the round tower survives. The pentagonal tower, standing 50m apart from the round one, is considerably less damaged. It has retained two (out of the original three) storeys. It could be entered both from ground level and the wall-walk. The two surviving storeys are pierced by slits. The destroyed upper storey possibly had windows and was designed for mounting artillery. There is a postern near the pentagonal tower, so narrow (0.55–0.6m wide) that a soldier wearing armour could only pass through it with difficulty. One characteristic of the fortifications at Oenoanda is the difference in the type of masonry on the frontal (outer) and inner sides: the latter is isodomic ashlar, while the former uses polygonal blocks.

Pednelissus (Pisidia)

Near Kozan village and the River Eurymedon (Köprüçay), 10km east of Kizillik Köy. The fortifications were probably built soon after 133 BC. They comprise a so-called acropolis, the lower city and a small section of a wall in the depression between the northern and central peaks of a ridge neighbouring the city. The 6m-high acropolis walls are crowned with a low parapet 0.72m high and 0.42m wide. Three surviving towers in the lower town are of particular interest. One is a gate-tower. It is adorned with two ornamental string-courses. Another tower was placed in such a way as to allow enfilade to be brought to bear upon the enemy along the walls on all four sides. Finally, the third tower is unique in surviving to its full height, 10.7m. Its uppermost storey has four small windows. Ruins of a guardhouse can be seen on the top of the northern crest.

Pergamon/Pergamum (Mysia)

Modern Bergama. One of the largest cities in Asia Minor, and the capital of the kingdom (282–133 BC), Pergamon was originally fortified in the 5th–4th centuries BC. These fortifications were built on the acropolis and later expanded on the south side by Philetairos (282–263 BC). It was, however, under Eumenes II (197–159 BC), who erected new, *c.* 4km-long city walls with towers and gates, that Pergamon received its most formidable fortifications. Ruins of these walls can still be seen in some places, as, for example, in the ruins of a tower at the entrance to the acropolis. However, most of the defensive walls that can be seen on the site today were built from stone, broken tiles and mortar, and date from the Byzantine period.

Perge (Pamphylia)

Located 2km north of Aksu village, near Antalya, a full description of Perge can be found in the chapter entitled 'A Tour of the Sites'.

Priene (Ionia)

Near modern Gullubahçe, about 15km from Söke. The fortifications built in the 4th century BC, in all probability after 334, protect the acropolis crowning the top of a rock and the city below. Their total length is about 2.5km, including 600m of acropolis walls. Today the walls are 8m high at most, but the parapet is no longer there – so the height of the walls probably must have reached 10m. The walls are dotted with 30 towers standing from 60 to 300m apart from each other; there are 17 towers in the lower town and 13 in the acropolis. A zigzag-shaped projection can occasionally be found in

The fortifications at the entrance to the acropolis of Pergamon. On the left are the ruins of a tower built from isodomic ashlar – one of the few remaining examples of the fortifications built in the early 2nd century BC by Eumenes II. The walls on the right of the tower were made from roughly worked stones alternating with broken tiles using mortar; these fortifications date back to the Byzantine period.

The fortifications of Priene were erected in the 4th century BC, supposedly after Alexander the Great's march across Asia Minor in 334 BC. About 30 towers protected the walls of the acropolis and the city lying below. One of them is shown in this photograph.

place of a tower. The towers used to have two storeys, but the second storeys have been all but lost. Three gates led into the lower city, a further one led into the acropolis. All the gates are in very poor condition.

Side (Pamphylia)
Located near Manavgat, a full description of Side can be found in the chapter entitled 'A Tour of the Sites'.

Sillyon (Pamphylia)
Located near Yanköy village, not far from Antalya, a full description of Sillyon can be found in the chapter entitled 'A Tour of the Sites'.

The main gate of Sillyon. This gate, consisting of two flanking towers with a semicircular courtyard behind them, represents a type very common in Pamphylia. A postern was made in the right-hand tower, which the defenders could use for a surprise attack upon the enemy.

A SUMMARY OF GREEK FORTIFICATIONS IN ASIA MINOR

Site	Date of the fortifications	Style of masonry	Curtains		Number and type of surviving towers	Other features
			Structure	Thickness (m)		
Alabanda (Caria)	4th–3rd centuries BC	C ash./trap.	'sandwich'	2.5–3.0	30 (28 rectangular, 1 pentagonal and 1 round)	jogs
Alinda (Caria)	4th century BC, before c. 340 C	C ash.	'sandwich'	2.20–2.25	19 (all are rectangular)	jogs (acropolis), postern
Amos (Caria)	early 4th century BC, later repaired	U pol., U ash.	'sandwich'	1.80	5 (all are rectangular)	
Assos (Troad)	6th century BC (?), 4th–3rd centuries BC	U pol./lesb.,U ash., C ash.	'sandwich', 'hollow' (tower)	2.40–3.65	12 (11 rectangular and 1 half-round)	
Cadyanda (Lycia)	late 3rd–2nd century BC	U pol. (wall), C ash. (buttresses)	'sandwich'	1.20 (+1.20m buttress = 2.40)		Buttresses behind the wall, salient
Caunos (Caria)	6th–4th centuries BC, some later changes	U pol./lesb., C ash., U ash./trap.	'sandwich'	2.15 2.40	6 (all are rectangular)	
Cnidus (Caria)	c. 330 BC	C ash., U pol.	'sandwich'	1.40–2.80 (in general >2.5), east wall c. 4.80	61 rectangular and 2 half-round	posterns
Colophon (Ionia)	late 4th century BC (probably 313–306 BC)	CC ash./trap., U pol./trap.	'sandwich'	2.15–2.35	14 (9 half-round, 1 round, the rest are rectangular)	salient, jogs
Ephesus (Ionia)	c. 290 BC	U trap., C ash.	'sandwich'	2.60–3.00	42/48	16 posterns, crenellated parapet, engine windows in towers, jogs
Erythrae (Ionia)	330–315 BC	C ash.	'sandwich'	3.50–5.20	4 (all are rectangular)	jogs, salient (50m wide), posterns
Halicarnassus (Caria)	mid-4th century BC	U pol. and trap., C ash.	'sandwich'	2.6 (limestone) 1.9–2.0 (granite)	18–27 (all are rectangular)	postern?
Heracleia on Latmus (Caria/Ionia)	c. 300 BC (Heracleia I), mid-3rd century BC (Heracleia II)	C ash.		2.00–3.30	65 (Heracleia I), 50 (Heracleia II)	19 gates and posterns, jogs, *epalxis*
Iasus (Caria) Mainland wall	turn of the 3rd/2nd centuries BC	U rubble		1.75–2.00	18 (all are half-round)	32 jogs, 68 posterns (about 150 for a full circuit, if it ever existed), slits for arrow-firing devices
Loryma III (Caria)	3rd or 2nd century BC	C ash.	'sandwich'	2.30–2.40	11 (2 round and 9 rectangular)	Laid using huge blocks, numerous posterns, small towers
Myndos (Caria)	between 367 and 334 BC	U pol., C ash.		2.75		
Oenoanda (Lycia)	between 188 and 159	C ash., U pol.	'sandwich'	1.70–1.80	2 (pentagonal and round)	
Pednelissus (Pisidia)	after 133 BC	C ash.	solid stone	1.60	3 (all are rectangular, one of them is a gate-tower)	gate-tower
Perge (Pamphylia)	c. 225 BC	C ash.	solid stone	1.40 or 2.00 (+1.20m buttress = 3.20)		artillery towers and curtains, a curtain with buttresses and mural gallery, few posterns
Priene (Ionia)	4th century BC, probably after 334	ash./trap.	'sandwich'	c. 2.0	30	epalxis, jogs (*crémaillère*)
Side (Pamphylia)	between 225 and 188 BC	C ash.	solid stone	3.00 or 1.70 (+1.40m buttress = 3.10)	13 (11 rectangular, 1 round and 1 half-round)	3 curtains of different structure, 3 levels of fighting in curtains, no posterns, *epalxis*
Sillyon (Pamphylia)	after 133	C ash./trap.	solid stone, 'hollow'	0.60–1.20		gate tower, battlements, fortified street and a fort at the entrance to a fortified street

Key to abbreviations/terms:
C – coursed; U – uncoursed; ash. – ashlar; lesb. – Lesbian; pol. – polygonal; trap. – trapezoidal; 'sandwich' – two faces of wall with rubble/earth filling in between; 'hollow' – without filling.

GLOSSARY

Acropolis   (Greek: 'high city') The citadel of a city.

Ballista   The term was used by the Romans for a torsion-powered double-armed stone-projector. In the Middle Ages the term was used for large, heavy, tension-powered (giant) crossbows and sometimes for hand crossbows.

Catapult   (Latin: *catapulta*, from the Greek *katapeltis*) A throwing machine. Initially (at least until the mid-1st century AD) the term stood for a torsion-powered arrow-firer only; later on the term was also applied to stone projectors.

Crémaillère   Jog or system of jogs (indented trace) facing the same direction and designed for the enfilade of curtains from one side only. Compare this with the '*saw-tooth trace*'.

Curtain   A section of wall between two towers.

Diateichisma   A cross-wall, which cuts through a section of an enceinte.

Diodoi   A system of avenues between the *proteichisma* and the main wall.

Emplecton   The meaning of this term, found only in an obscure passage of Vitruvius [2.8.7], is not quite clear. Some scholars believe that it means the structure of a wall consisting of two faces with rubble in between, whilst others refer it to header-and-stretcher masonry.

Epalxion   A parapet, usually crenellated.

Epalxis   A continuous parapet pierced with slits or windows, not crenellated (before the 4th century BC *epalxis* refers to a crenellated parapet, though).

Euthytone   An arrow-firer.

Gastraphetes   (Greek: 'belly-bow') An ancient Greek crossbow that fired short bolts (40–60cm). Sometimes the term *gastraphetes* was also used for a non-torsion-powered throwing machine on a stand (e.g. Biton).

Geländemauer   ('The great circuit') A far-reaching circuit with defensive walls encircling a large piece of territory to include all the heights into the defences. The fortifications are not conditioned by the area actually occupied and large uninhabited grounds find themselves inside the city walls.

Hypostasis   The lower part of a parapet.

Katastegasma   A roof over the *epalxis*.

Lithobolos	The full Greek name is *katapeltes lithobolos*, but the first word (catapult) was often omitted – a missile-throwing machine, adapted for projecting stones.
Oxybeles	The full Greek name is *katapeltes oxybeles*, but again the first word (catapult) was often omitted – an ancient Greek missile-throwing machine. The tension model appeared about 375 BC, then (between 353 and 341 BC) a torsion-powered version of this machine was invented. Some of its varieties shot bolts, others fired small stone balls.
Palinton	A stone-projector.
Parodos	A wall-walk.
Phrourion	A fort, designed exclusively for a military garrison (*phroura*).
Polybolos	A repeating arrow-firer invented by Dionysius of Alexandria around the mid-3rd century BC.
Postern	A sally-port, or small gateway designed primarily for a sudden sortie and counter-attack.
Promacheones	Merlons, battlements or a parapet in general.
Proteichisma	An outwork.
'Saw-tooth trace'	Sharp bends in a wall – a system of jogs (indented trace) – facing the enemy with a sharp angle, and allowing for the enfilade of curtains in two directions. Compare with *crémaillère*.
Testudo	(Latin: 'tortoise') Roman fighting order with soldiers protecting themselves with shields at the front, on the sides and above; the formation was used when assaulting fortifications.
Tyrsis	A private residential tower or fortified farmstead; a keep.

The main or West Gate at Assos. The gate proper, revealed by false pointed arches at the front and at the back, has been destroyed. However, two rectangular towers flanking the gate are fairly well preserved. The left-hand one is 16m high, and only has slits on the second floor. There are two corbels with square sockets above the slits. Flags may have been placed in these sockets. The towers had battlements, evidenced by a now lost drainage gutter in the upper course.

BIBLIOGRAPHY AND FURTHER READING

Adam, J.–P., *L'Architecture militaire grecque* (Paris, 1982)

Aineias Tacticus, *How to Survive under Siege* (Oxford, 1990)

Benddorf, O., and Niemann, G., *Reisen in Lykien und Karien* (*Reisen im süd-westlichen Kleinasien*, I) (Vienna, 1884)

Camp, J. M., 'Notes on the towers and borders of classical Boiotia', *American Journal of Archaeology*, 95 (1991), pp. 193–202

Cooper, F. A., 'Epaminondas and Greek fortifications', *American Journal of Archaeology*, 90 (1986), pp. 195–205

Fortificationes Antiquae, Ottawa Conference 1983 (Amsterdam, 1992)

Garlan, Y., 'Fortifications et histoire grecque' in *Problèmes de la guerre en Grèce ancienne* (Paris, 1968)

Garlan, Y., *Recherches de poliorcétique grecque* (Paris, 1974)

von Gerkan, A., *Griechische Städteanlagen* (Berlin, 1924)

von Gerkan, A., *Milet*, II, 3: *Die Stadtmauern*, ed. T. Wiegand (Berlin, 1935)

Judeich, W., *Kleinasiatische Studien* (Marburg, 1892)

Karlsson, L., *Fortification Towers and Masonry Techniques of Syracuse 405–211 BC* (Stockholm, 1992)

Kern, P. B., *Ancient Siege Warfare* (London, 1999)

Krischen, F., 'Die Befestigungen von Herakleia am Latmos' in *Milet*, III.2 (Berlin, 1922)

La Fortification dans L'Histoire du Monde Grec, Actes de Colloque International: Valbonne 1982 (Paris, 1986)

Lanckoronski, K. (ed.), *Städte Pamphyliens und Pisidiens*, 2 Vols. (Vienna, 1890–92)

Lawrence, A. W., *Greek Aims in Fortification* (Oxford, 1979)

Lawrence, A. W., *Greek Architecture* (Harmondsworth, 1983)

Livy, *The History of Rome* (London, 1905)

Maier, F. G., *Griechische Maurbauinschriften*, Vols. I–II (Heidelberg, 1959–61)

Marsden, E. W., *Greek and Roman Artillery: Historical Development* (Oxford, 1999)

McNicoll, A. W., and Winikoff, T., 'A Hellenistic fortress in Lycia: The Isian Tower?' *American Journal of Archaeology*, 87 (1983), pp. 311–23

McNicoll, A. W., 'Developments in techniques of siegecraft and fortifications in the Greek world ca. 400–100 BC' in *La Fortification dans L'Histoire du Monde Grec* (Paris, 1986), pp. 305–13

McNicoll, A. W., *Hellenistic Fortifications: From the Aegean to the Euphrates* (Oxford, 1997). This is the most highly recommended book on Greek fortifications in Asia Minor.

Nossov, K., *Ancient and Medieval Siege Weapons: A Fully Illustrated Guide to Siege Weapons and Tactics* (Guildford, 2005)

Ober, J., 'Early artillery towers: Messenia, Boiotia, Attica, Megarid', *American Journal of Archaeology*, 91 (1987), pp. 569–604

The Oxford Encyclopedia of Archaeology in the Near East, Vols. 1–5 (New York and Oxford, 1997)

Paton, W. R., and Myres, J. L., 'Karian sites and inscriptions', *Journal of Hellenic Studies*, 16 (1896), pp. 188–271

Philon, *Belopoeica*, in Marsden, E. W., *Greek and Roman Artillery: Technical Treatises* (Oxford, 1999)

Philon, *Poliorketika*, in Lawrence, A. W., *Greek Aims in Fortification* (Oxford, 1979)

Scranton, R. L., *Greek Walls* (Cambridge, MA: Harvard University Press, 1941)

Wiegand, T., and Schrader, H., *Priene* (Berlin, 1904)

Wiegand, T. (ed.), *Milet*, Vol. I– (Berlin, 1906–) (excavations continue)

Winter, F. E., *Greek Fortifications* (London, 1971)

INDEX

References to illustrations are shown in **bold**. Plates are shown with page and caption locators in brackets.